# TALES FROM THE HIGH LONESOME

## Volume 3

Written by L. Scott Hancock

Copyright © 2025 L. Scott Hancock

ISBN (Hardback): 979-8-89381-124-7
ISBN (Paperback): 979-8-89381-125-4
ISBN (eBook): 979-8-89381-126-1

All rights reserved. No part of this book may be reproduced or transmitted in any form or by any means, electronic or mechanical, including photocopying, recording, or by any information storage and retrieval system, without permission in writing from the copyright owner.

The views expressed in this work are solely those of the author and do not necessarily reflect the views of the publisher, and the publisher hereby disclaims any responsibility for them.

508 West 26th Street KEARNEY, NE 68848
402-819-3224
info@medialiteraryexcellence.com

# Contents

Dedication ................................................................................ 1
Hands ...................................................................................... 2
"AND A GOOD TIME WAS HAD BY ALL" ................... 5
"It's A Wonderful Life" ........................................................ 8
Captain Eric ......................................................................... 12
Ezra And Jody ..................................................................... 15
Kesler's and "Mom and Pops" ........................................... 18
Roots and Roses .................................................................. 21
Working ............................................................................... 24
Sport Shop Dreams ............................................................. 27
Under The Big Top ............................................................. 31
A Teacher to Remember .................................................... 34
Drugstore Cowboys ............................................................ 38
Freedom Phil ....................................................................... 41
P.O. Box K ............................................................................ 44
World Series Flu ................................................................. 47
A Week ................................................................................. 50
Cleanup and Trish .............................................................. 53
What's Right ........................................................................ 56
T. Bird ................................................................................... 59
America's Longest Main Street ......................................... 63
'Dubby' ................................................................................. 67
Father Tim ........................................................................... 71
Auntie Pat ............................................................................ 74
Last Chance ......................................................................... 77
Ross Park and The Drive-In .............................................. 80
Freya, Jessie, Horses and Love .......................................... 84
Brain Sweeping ................................................................... 89
Common Threads and Ken ............................................... 92

| | |
|---|---|
| Is A Camel A HORSE? | 96 |
| Mary M | 99 |
| Spring Forward and Elisa | 103 |
| Parking Decorum | 107 |
| Shadow People | 110 |
| Winter Story | 113 |
| More Boots, Less Beans | 116 |
| Up In Smoke | 120 |
| Parking Lot Wonders | 124 |
| Shorty's Scouts | 127 |
| Wonderments | 130 |
| Molly B' Damn and Wyatt | 133 |
| Pump Handle and the Wagon | 136 |
| Truefitt & Hill, Est. 1805 | 139 |
| Now, It's Fall | 142 |
| Rest In Peace | 146 |
| Story Time | 149 |
| One of A Kind | 153 |
| "Rhythm of the Rails" | 157 |
| Poky and the Iron Road | 161 |
| Trees and Other Friends | 165 |
| Red Wings and Spring | 168 |
| Sweet Surprises | 171 |
| About the Author | 176 |

*Tales from the High Lonesome*

# Dedication

Dr. Roger Rowse, visionary, seeker, universal thinker and healer.
Blackfoot, Idaho
December 2024


Cover artwork created by Gordon Perry, Pocatello, Idaho.
Western artist, historian, vintage firearms expert, and Mountain Man.
A special thank you to Lewis and Clark Traders, Lewiston, Idaho, for allowing us to use the artwork

# Hands

The other day, while watching my nephew and wife move firewood Fidel the Woodman had delivered, I looked down at one of my hands resting on the fence.

It was my father's hand from long ago when I last looked at those hands that were slimming down with more knuckle showing as age slowly changed the vice grip of before to a more agreeable grasp. Those hands that had completed a million tasks in his 84 years. Hands that held a baby as gently as his rock-hard grip held a sledgehammer, the change had come on slowly as the majority of his years were behind him. As we fished together for the last time, up the north fork of the Coeur d'Alene River, I drifted through the hundreds of hours we had spent together on some of the West's greatest streams. His spinning rod had replaced his bamboo fly rod, as his ability to wade the waters he loved diminished while presenting a fly. He still fly-fished, but not nearly as often as in his early married years. His hand on the fluted fore stock of his trusted vintage 870 shotgun was one that is indelible, as I sit here writing. He loved to hunt the winged masters of the southeast Idaho sky. Pheasants were his favorite. We hunted deer and elk to put meat on the table, and I once saw him kill a running bull elk with a bolt action 30-30 in one shot. Today, all the big bore magnum buffs would scoff at such an attempt. To him, it was food for his family against the long, brutal East Idaho winters. He was a wing shooter, and he was very good. His love of the field in fall was accentuated by my mother's love of being out in the farm country, in stubble fields or sagebrush. She would park the old Chevy behind any nearby haystack, to get us out of the ever-present southern Idaho wind. As the old six banger settled down under the hood, Mother would bring out lunch and coffee for Dad and my brothers as they hunted the field toward us. I waited on the edge haystack hoping for a flyby rooster with my brothers' Sears and Roebuck 20 gauge. A lady friend of mine in North Idaho once asked how I hunted pheasants. It wasn't complicated; I waited at the end of a field or on the edge. Pheasants fly straight, even if towards a hunter. Many of my shots were incoming or straightaways, as our old Labrador pushed them toward me. Some were flybys that I had learned to lead, out of necessity. As I drift back now, I remember Mother's hands in her late years. Still strong, but they showed the hard farm work, cooking years during the war at the Pocatello Army airfield, and countless other tasks from house painting to being the best baker around. Her hands were very large for a woman, but she was a large woman, 5' 10" in her youth and skinny as a rail. Those same hands held babies with all the love she could muster. Her love of babies and children could not be overstated. Mother always cried when she saw a TV ad describing the hardships of children in less favorable conditions, and those same hands grabbed a Kleenex to dab tears streaming down her cheeks. Arriving at her bedside in Salt Lake, where she had been flown after a brain hemorrhage, she was gripping bedsheets, her ring made of birthstones of all her children still adorning her finger. Her strong hands held on till the end. I gripped them many times during those few days, and she responded with a firm grasp.

Looking down on my own hand resting on the fence, the thought of how good they had served me over these many years was clear. I have been fortunate all my life to have the gift of good hands, with adequate strength to get me from one place to another on crutches or in my wheelchair. A few years back a doctor asked, as he held a hand, if I had much pain with my arthritic fingers. My reply was, "They are not arthritic. Those big knuckles and strong fingers are from years of making up for other body parts that were not as useful after polio, and thank God, they have served me so well."

I was told she was unresponsive as I entered my dear friend Mary McFarland's room at Bonner General in Sandpoint. As I reached down to take hold of one of her 95-year-old hands, Sarah, her daughter smiled. The years replayed in my mind of all the construction jobs I had done on their one of kind, river delta ranch out of Clark Fork. She and Glenn had been my friends for almost fifty years. As I picked up the nearest calloused hand, a hand that had driven countless motorcycles all over the world, flown thousands of miles as a pilot, hands that had farmed and ranched for 85 years, I whispered to her, "Mary, it's Scott." I felt the strong grip I remembered for all those years. She knew it was me.

As a boy in the Elks Rehabilitation Hospital in Boise, Mother brought me a book filled with black and white photographs of the world's greatest sculptures. As I thumbed through the pages, the hand of David, Michelangelo's masterpiece in Florence, Italy, held me spellbound. It still does. Look and understand, all the answers are there, in that divine hand from a Master's hand.

# "... And A Good Time Was Had by All"

There were many years of my life when I tried repeatedly to find land that suited me in the Salmon area. Salmon, Idaho, has been in my brain for as long as I can remember. I did find places that were to my liking on two occasions. In both cases, I put money down only to learn later, with title searches, that water rights were not guaranteed, a sad but not unusual surprise. When deeds were originally filed back in the late 1800s, they left specifics out quite often on purpose. The law of the West and land sales back then were unclear on absolutes when a bargain sale was afoot. During this searching period I took the *Salmon Herald* newspaper, to my great delight. This local gem of a paper had columns from around the county, written by locals who gave the news as they saw it. Down home reportage with local slants that made the whole thing worthwhile. One of the columns was from Gibsonville, down river from Salmon. I think the eatery there was called the Lewis and Clark. It seems plausible as it was the exact route the "Party of Discovery" took when exploring the west and finding their way over the mountains with Sacajawea as their salvation, guiding them through her homeland.

The Gibsonville columnist would put in an article about the locals having their weekly confab at the café. She would tell of all who attended and what fun they had, and every column ended with "and a good time was had by all."

My mother, when questioned by her grandkids as to how folks found entertainment when she was young, came back with the same answer every time: "We made our own fun with whatever we were doing or what was available."

I've thought a lot about that lately. Why is everyone so miserable and seemingly lost as to enjoyment? I don't think it's just this god-awful disease we're all bludgeoned with every day from every angle; it's larger than that. The world seems to be adrift in a sea of ennui. Is it lack of personal respect and foundation? Daily, the TV talking heads tell us how to feel about things that have transpired around us. The news media focuses on their idea of what our health and, more importantly, our mental health is about and what direction it is headed. We become more frightened with each passing minute when mountebanks lecture us on everything and anything. What we really need is independence of thought and, encouragement to find our own 'good times'. We have fallen into a hypnotic state, with a lack of political guidance that is proposed to be the answer, when in fact they have no answers. The answers are personal and alive in our brains, waiting to be released.

I read a recent article by Deepak Chopra, the Indian MD writer and guru of all things sacred. His message was simple; "We need an epidemic of joy." Sound simple? Maybe it is simple, so simple we are the ones that must control it!

My friend Dr. Roger called while I was writing this, which is not unusual. He rings in whenever I am deep in thought, trying to make sense of what I am saying. Somehow the energy waves tell him I'm in trouble making a plausible situation sound and available. Dr. Roger is a health practitioner, retired, and a beloved friend and guide, not a yuppie phony spewing silliness. Roger thinks it all starts with losing a personal foundation to bolster us. This pushed me back to thoughts about Mother's wisdom. She thought a good foundation for making it in the public arena was the two magic words; "Please" and "Thank You." Works for me!

I went to a funeral this past week and I was shocked at the service. Rather than talking about the good life the person had led it became a therapeutic indulgence for those speaking, addressing their own commitment to God. I respect their right to embrace any faith they choose, but rather than personal sanctimony I wanted to hear about the person in the casket, and their good works while still on top of the sod. I wanted to hear about the people they touched, and *their* service to mankind.

I speak to people each day with their own "sack of rocks," trying to make it down life's path. Never sure what to say in the way of good advice, I stumble along telling them all the polite things I learned from my parents, relatives and people I grew up with. I ask these friends in need to believe in themselves, and the possibility of change in the course of their life. Nothing more, nothing less. The most successful people I have known had self-control and a dollop of luck in building their lives, often against overwhelming odds. As Warren Buffet has extolled, "The most important thing to learn for a successful life is when to say NO." That includes to the talking heads. Turn off the tube and take a walk or read a book. Another important thing, in my book, is to know when to say YES to yourself, and to build on whatever strengths you have. Try to find some joy in the day, something significant no matter how small it may be. For me, it's watching the birds at my winter feeder while sipping coffee. I hear their reporters, the Magpies, say after they do ground cleanup below, "and a good time was had by all."

*L. Scott Hancock*

# "It's A Wonderful Life"

I am a great admirer of this Jimmy Stewart movie set in a Christmas town, somewhere in an imaginary America. If you have not seen this 1946 classic, I suggest you find a copy and watch it. It will warm your heart to the promise of a better tomorrow. "It's a Wonderful Life" is also the name of a famous photo by Idaho's genius photographer from the past, Ross Hall. I tell folks often in my writings that North and South Idaho are almost like two different states. The residents of the South don't know much about North Idaho unless they have lived there, or have relatives they visited in the Panhandle. South Idaho knowledge of Ross Hall is a prime example. I knew of Ross as I grew up, when family friends would send me postcards in the rehab center I stayed at in Boise, which had Ross Hall scenic photos covering the front of the cards. I read everything I could about him, and the fact this famous Eastman Kodak Co.-celebrated photographer lived in the north lands of my home state.

Ross Hall's son Dann recently died. Dann was a friend and a great photographer in his own right. Dann ran Hallan's Gallery, on First Avenue in Sandpoint, where they reproduced digitally updated photos from the thousands of negatives Ross left behind. I have one hanging in my hall, titled "Teddy and Bo." The picture shows an old man with his cocker spaniel over his shoulder, laying back in his boat, bamboo fishing rod in hand, smoking his curved pipe while floating along on Lake Pend Oreille. A famous photograph, with hundreds of copies on adorning walls across the world. Mine was a gift from Dann. My friend Bobby in Hope, Idaho still owns the fishing pole shown in the photo. Ross Hall photographs made the pages of countless magazines of the era, including ten front covers of Life Magazine. When the Navy set up its training base at the south end of Lake Pend Oreille, Ross was the man the Navy picked to do their photographic history. Eastman Kodak officials told Navy brass they had one of the best photographers anywhere living in nearby Sandpoint. Ross's period photographs give an intimate view into this famous Naval base at Farragut State Park. The Farragut Naval Station still works with underwater submarine technology because the lake is deep enough to provide ocean-like conditions. It makes people blink twice when I tell them Idaho has an active Naval base!

Ross and Hazel Hall set up shop in Sandpoint, on First Avenue, and produced thousands of the most remarkable photographs. Pictures equal to other giants of photography, Ansel Adams or Alfred Stieglitz. Ross was a genius who would go to any length to produce images that would stand the test of time. I once remarked that I grew up looking at huge reproductions of Indian Chiefs of Idaho adorning the walls of the Whitman Hotel coffee shop in old Pocatello. Dann, nor Hazel, were aware of their existence or how they got there. Professionally trained as a photographer, Ross understood the hardships involved in making a once in a lifetime shot. He hiked to the tops of peaks on snowshoes, put himself up a tree or out on a rock precipice, or any other precarious stand necessary to make a great picture and a lasting image of his art. All while carrying heavy loads of photographic apparatus on his back.

By the time I got to know Ross, the limelight was starting to dim in his eyes, but I gleaned from him what it took to make a good photograph: Commitment. My firsthand knowledge of Ross came from my dear friend, legendary Lake Captain Fred

Kennedy, who was partly responsible for many of the lake photos, manning the helm of boats while Ross shot film. Ross and Hazel stood up for Fred and Lottie at their wedding.

Fred's stories were historic to me. Imagine a kid in a hospital later meeting the man responsible for the photographs on postcards he received while there. I relayed this story to Ross once, and he smiled. No more kind and gentle soul lived than Ross. Tall and trim, he was a willow in the wind. His works are part of countless museum and photography displays, with Eastman Kodak Co. proclaiming at one time, "Ross Hall is one of the ten best photographers alive!"

I have seen hundreds of Ross Hall's pictures, and that's barely the surface. For the admirers of his works, we still have much to look forward to, as his negatives are still being discovered and reproduced. The Hallans Gallery in Sandpoint will go on. It is my understanding the gallery will continue in the hands of a well-trained, faithful follower of Ross's work. For this I am overwhelmingly grateful; his work needs to live and enlighten forever. This master of photographic technique brought us indelible images that will survive well beyond the current craze for his work. And that is as it should be.

Photos: A pencil rendering of Ross's famous Christmas photo of bygone Sandpoint: "It's A Wonderful Life."

Congressman Larry LaRocco and Me. Sandpoint, 1990. Photo: Dann Hall.

# Captain Eric

The deck of the old Tobler Marina Café was uncommonly hot as we sat under our awning, sipping iced tea waiting for lunch. The Marina, located on North Idaho's famous Hayden Lake, was crowded with boaters waiting to launch in hopes of leaving the sweltering heat. Lunch arrived with a cooling breeze coming off the lake, and the day was good again. As I recall, I heard the voices of teenagers splashing and yelling before I saw what looked like an old Navy lifeboat loaded with young revelers enjoying everything about their float on the lake. I remember a lunch party member commenting, "Wow! That looks like fun." Little did I know the leader of the boat party would come into my life soon after. Sandpoint, its ski area, and Lake Pend Oreille would become his home for the next stretch of the adventure in his still young life. As a boy, he once told his mother, "When I grow up, if you want to visit me, you will have to sleep in a hammock." True to his word, his mother had this experience and many more. Eric once wrote, "In my heart, I have always been a sailor." I'm sure it is true; he first went to sea as a fisherman with the Alaskan fleet. From the beginning Eric was an adventurer, an explorer on a life quest. He rode his bike to the Bay Area from North Idaho early on, and had countless early encounters with the world at large; it was his arena. At one point in time, his mother had no idea where he was in the world, except for occasional cards from China, Russia, Tibet, or some other far-off place in the Himalayas. He was gone over a year on this junket, ending up walking to our front door in Twin Lakes as though he had just been away for a few days. His mother learned how to cope with these extended, worrisome trips, and while he sailed much of the earth with his friend Joe, she waited for word from different ports across the globe as the trip progressed.

The hardest part for me writing about Eric is knowing where to start, what adventures to include and where to stop. His life has been anything but ordinary. A trip to help a relative in Florida started his life on the seas more permanently. First as a paramedic, then as a tug boat deck hand in Key West. As a paramedic, he applied with the Japanese team competing in the Paris to Dakar, a desert 4x4 auto race. This experience led to his long-time association with Dr. Franck Goddio, one of the world's pre-eminent underwater archeologists and founder of the Institut Européen d' Archeologie Sous-Marine in Paris. As a research diver with Dr. Goddio, Eric has years of underwater exploration in Alexandria Harbor, Egypt. Beneath the waves lie some of the world's greatest treasures from the ancients. Earthquakes and floods sunk these cultural marvels centuries ago. Goddio and his team have explored and mapped these sunken treasures for over twenty years, bringing up statues and other artifacts to be catalogued, filmed, and then lowered back into place at the bottom of the harbor, as Egyptian law dictates. Their explorations have been documented by film crews and TV networks from across the globe. "Cleopatra's Lost Palace" was one of the most viewed TV presentations, garnering a worldwide audience. More recently, the team has been exploring the lost city of Heracleion, also below the waves off Egypt's north shore, in Aboukir Harbor. Eric now captains the *Princess Duda* exploration ship, owned by the research team sponsors. Each year, he flies to Malta, where the ship is berthed, and prepares it to navigate the Mediterranean en route to the dive points in Egypt.

To speak of Eric, one must acknowledge that he holds an

International Explorers Card. This globally recognized document helps ensure the holder's safety in hostile situations. Once, off the coast of Egypt, their expedition ship was boarded by pirates at night while in the harbor, and had to be rescued by the Egyptian Navy!

Eric's travels and gifts are shared with diverse groups online and in person. He lectures widely, including to the Spokane, WA, Archeological Society. His talks are met with resounding enthusiasm. World travels have brought him into contact with other fascinating professions he embraced and incorporated into his resume as time permitted. In the off-season, when not in Egypt, he may be found captaining a "jack up" construction barge under a bridge in the Hudson River, or using a magnetic field apparatus to locate bomb ordinance left from the Vietnam War in Cambodia. The High Lakes expedition, sponsored by NASA in the Andes Mountains, was an unbelievable opportunity for him and his historical talents.

Key West has been Eric and wife Teresa's home for a long time, giving them access to some of the world's great waters, gifted divers, explorers and marine scientists. Teresa maintains the solid ground, as Eric's onsite jobs can keep him away for months at a time. I encourage the reader to look up any number of sites on the internet that have Eric's adventures encapsulated, including his experience with his own scientific vessel, the *Ketty Lund*. Visit: Captain Eric Wartenweiler Smith@discoverer.com. In 2000 Eric's mother and I visited Eric and Teresa in Key West, a trip I shall never forget. My wife spoke of this trip with warm remembrance just before her death in 2017. Watching the sun go down over the water from Mallory Square is an unforgettable visual delight I can see before my eyes to this day.

# Ezra and Jody

In the 1950s, my brothers walked from the beautiful old Union Pacific train depot on the hill in Boise all the way out 25th Street to Sycamore Drive and the Elk's Rehabilitation Center, where I resided. Walking, instead of taking a cab, gave them more money to buy presents for me, as they stopped at stores along the way. It took about an hour and a half to walk the five-plus miles. Riding from Pocatello using Dad's railroad pass, they came at least once a month when the folks simply had to attend to other obligations and gave them a break from their almost weekly trips. In those days it was near a seven-hour rail ride, with all the mail and milk stops in every little burg with any population. On one visit, Lorin, my older poet brother, gave me a small poetry book. In it were poets of the world, including Idaho's Ezra Pound. I was young, but I read and reread every page in the evening after mess in the dinner hall. Polio had turned the old veterans' home barracks on Sycamore Drive into a rehab center for those afflicted. My total time spent there gave me near-Boise residency of more than five years, off and on.

The poetry book was a step up from my Golden Books containing simple works of Americana. I think, if memory serves, I lent the book to a girl I was madly in love with, as madly as one can be at twelve, and then she was released from the rehab center, breaking my heart and purloining my book forever. From the day Ezra Pound was introduced until I studied him in college under Geoffrey Palmer, he confounded and intrigued me with his genius and skill in creating symbols with words that were almost clairvoyant. I cannot tell you how

Pound writes, I lack the ability, but it is clear his Imagist Style led the American and English style in the Modernist Movement.

Born in Hailey, Idaho, in 1885, just downstream from Hemingway's residence (much later) in the Wood River Valley, Pound was not subject to Idaho influences that our other native Idaho writing genius, Vardis Fisher, was. The Pound family left Idaho when he was four. Early in his adulthood he went to Paris, then Italy, living a very interesting and troubling life, but his mark on poetry and literature is chiseled in granite. Hemingway, Faulkner, W.B. Yeats, Robert Frost, D.H. Lawrence, and T.S. Eliot were among hundreds of admirers and stylists using Pound as a foundation for their own creative bent. His work is still confusing and somewhat vague to me, but I plug away at it at least once every year, hoping to understand his written word. I don't subscribe to what some biographers or PBS program tells me about what his prose and poetry really meant. Pound learned all the classic languages and read texts from the ages, rounding out his Modernist Movement standards for the Arts.

Enter Jody. For years, I read articles in the *River Journal* submitted by a writer named Jody Forrest from what he called the Surrealist Bureau. His work had a perimeter that I could cross at certain junctures when my brain allowed. I read his articles time and time again, knowing his writing had that aura I couldn't quite grasp, but I tried. I heard others say "that guy is just too weird for me," which only fueled my search for his hidden secret society of language. I thought someday the two of us would meet, but our paths never crossed in the county we shared. I learned from his sister he had a fairly abstract life. Not surprising to me, having read his work. His life included a tour in Vietnam, which in and of itself could create lasting surrealism. Recently, in writing an article about the editor of the

*River Journal* and my discussion with Trish (his sister) and the editor/publisher, it came to me like a clear bell on a quiet day. His writing was as oblique as was Pound's to my mind. Both held me in a spell I have not overcome.

Pound and Fisher were writing geniuses but difficult to absorb for the casual reader, or maybe not. After all, seeing through their eyes gives meaning to angles not encountered on a daily basis. Years ago, the *Idaho State Journal* published poems each week by a pioneer family's granddaughter. Nick Ifft, publisher of that paper, once told me why they were important: though a bit repetitive with predictable rhyming, they told a story. I applaud anyone who puts their work out for public scrutiny. But I have a request, Jody and Ezra, from your perch on high, please send me a missive telling me what the hell you were really saying so I can be at rest and continue analyzing Vardis Fisher's "Testament of Man." Oh, and Vardis, if you're listening from a cloud altar, send me some notes clarifying your thoughts. Most of us remain baffled after years of study.

L. Scott Hancock

# Kesler's and Mom and Pops

Bill gave us a penny candy when we came into his store on the corner of Maple and Willard Street in Pocatello in the 1950s. Bill's Handy Grocery was just half a block from my house, so Mother would send us down for last-minute canning supplies or meal items she was short on. Her last words as you went out the door were, "Tell Bill to put it on the bill." The phrase struck me so funny, but I understood: he was to add it to our monthly account, paid for on payday at the end of the month.

A recent thought about all of this made me reflect on a sadness that happened not long ago in Firth. The local market, The Stop-n-Shop, closed. I remember my first stop there in the 1970s. A cold beer was my reward after a hard day of work around the house on weekends. To my surprise, while working for Boise-Cascade in Idaho Falls, Sunday was a day of reflection, not beer drinking. Therefore, no spirits of any kind were sold in Bonneville County on the Lord's Day. To my amazement, just south into Bingham County, I could buy a six pack. Those days are gone, as are the days of the small Mom and Pop grocery stores across America. Today, the corporate giant food chains and the modern quick-stop stores are the store du jour.

When I moved to Sandpoint, Harold's Market was still the mainstay of the downtown community. Harold's had every misfit employee imaginable, but they all seemed to fit in with that downhome atmosphere. I loved Harold's and its unlevel floors and mid-'50s shelving. The bakery made the best gooey-coated tasties. A small adjoining café served soup and sandwich specials to many of the town's *special* people. Progress, which I often question, turned Harold's to dust, and a mega-banking operation moved in.

The good news is some Mom and Pops live on.

Dave's Jubilee in Ashton is a fine example, as one travels south after a weekend in Island Park or Yellowstone. Right on the highway, it holds just about everything needed for the long haul or a weekend camping trip to the Tetons. Products wedged into every available nook and cranny keep this family enterprise afloat.

As a child, Mother and I would shop for meats at Del Monte's in Pocatello. This legendary store still operates today, but without much in the grocery line. It has become primarily a meat and smoked meat purveyor for the surrounding region, including Island Park outlets and into Yellowstone. Colleen and I stop at its West Center Street hillside location a few times a year for smoked treats. I go there because I have been doing so at least once a year for as long as my memory remembers. Even when on visits home from North Idaho, Del Monte's was still on Mother's shopping list. She would ask me to "go pick up something nice for dinner."

BI-LO Grocery on 15th Street in Pocatello still operates the best little big store in town. Family owned and operated for many years, it serves the college community as well today as it did when I was a student at ISU. For folks who love pork, this is your place. Each year, they have special order pork roasts and other porcine delights that cannot be surpassed—a tradition they uphold to this day. Every so often, BI-LO offers canned goods by the case, which megastores would be hard-pressed to match in price.

"Hard work, family values, and customer relations" is the standard by which Kesler's Market in Blackfoot has made their success for 87 years. This family-owned and operated Gold Standard of locally owned family grocery stores has managed, in this day of corporate expanded food chains, to survive and thrive. Kesler's story is remarkable, from father to son and father to son again, it continues. Starting as a sixteen-by-twenty-foot log building, today, it occupies an entire block, with its adjoining garden store. Kesler's is a legend in the area, and it retains that local feeling of friendship and personal care for the customer. They will deliver your food and even install salt in your water conditioner with a smile and goodwill. Perhaps that's why they have survived customer relations, honest intent, and most of all, good manners toward all. In the corner of their lot, they have a neon retro sign that reads sometimes in winter, "Too cold to change the sign, we have groceries, come in." That says it all! This Christmas, Kesler's will sell us our Christmas tree, that comes from Morris Christmas Tree Farm in North Idaho, folks we know. I will continue to support these small local stores to keep them alive, if for nothing else but to keep them open for folks I see daily walking to their last neighborhood grocery to resupply their pantries.

I drive by the old buildings, now abandoned, dark, and empty, and still see the shelves filled with canned goods, with mercantile items like canvas, nails, shovels, and hoes. Stores that had a conscience for a sense of community that must exist for all to succeed and thrive.

# Roots and Roses

Gnarly old cottonwood roots crawl across the ground, forming a hump where a giant cottonwood rises. The roots come out of the ground, then return beneath the soil to rise again a few feet away. Looking ghostly as they reach forward, it seems somehow appropriate to this Halloween day. Colleen burns piles of golden orange leaves next to its base, part, and parcel to its having survived another summer clutching life, going into the long cold spell, re-emerging with buds in the not-too-far-off future. The tree and its roots create a small hillock in the backyard near the field, a hump I enjoy. It gives the lawn character. Nature is perfect, we are not in it. We cannot control the end which will come to us or the tree, and that makes me smile. Man and Nature are vulnerable; we need to learn that.

Out front, we still have flowers in bloom, undaunted by the recent snowstorm and cold snap. They are gorgeous. Our far-reaching white rose has two blossoms, and it's almost November. On the bench, under the awning covering the front porch, sits a geranium, blooming in loud profusion not recognizing it too must go into the garage for survival (if we're lucky). The white rose has branches as thick as my thumb and thorns like a toothpick, though shorter. After the blooms and the leaves have gone, the finches will land on these branches and wait their turn at the feeder. The cold season is coming. Like most folks, we try to prepare for any interruptions winter might provide. The snow tires are on.

Friends and family are reporting their fall hunting successes, with some fishing tales thrown in. We watched a fly fisherman near the interstate bridge in Blackfoot casting to the great Trout God, within spitting distance of semi-trucks and trailers going north to Butte or south to Salt Lake City or ports in between.

I have told you before I watch the waters, wondering where that flow in front of me will be tomorrow. It haunts me in a good way.

The window on the woodstove keeps me from climbing in. I fear the older I get I am more and more like Sam McGee, from Robert Service's great poem about Sam's cremation in the Yukon. My bones seem colder these days and fires more warming in heat and to my soul. The fleece blanket I have over me at night is just the ticket. I call her Sophia because it so warms me in the chilly darkness.

Today, as I lit the fire, I thought of yet another old friend that has left us. The mother of one of my former carpenters and a dear friend, she was everything America should be about. A grade school teacher, Sunday School teacher, and all-around marvelous example to us all. In this case, the old saying "they don't make them like that anymore" is ever so true. Like the cottonwood leaves, her time had come, and she lives in the sunsets.

This evening, a flock of geese flew over to alight on the winter wheat field next to the house. The Old Frankie Lane song, *I Want to Go Where the Wild Goose Goes*, came to mind. In truth, it would be nice to soar overhead, looking down for once instead of up. It made me wonder if geese think, "Wow, look at those grain fields," instead of us saying, "Wow, look at those clouds." I know it's a bit anthropomorphic but, what the hell, who cares?

Life is never pure with clear answers, and that's as it should be. Just when I think my age has given me a certain wisdom, life tells me differently. Clouds are memories to me, as are the waters and old friends, be they human or the soft furry type. Each carries its own truth, and from that truth, I gain the wisdom I need. Nothing passes without leaving a memory.

My friend Dennis reminds me how important words are. Words, and examples set by others, are what we navigate by. This could be a lesson for those bloated with ego and circumstance, lecturing all us "common folks" daily from their lofty towers of self-proclaimed excellence. We're all just folks trying to do the best with what we have and leave the world a better place. For those that have gone on recently, I salute you for trying and succeeding in doing just that. Of course, we'll miss you and rue the void you leave, but the memories of you and the roots and roses of life will live on to enlighten another day and a new generation.

L. Scott Hancock

# Working

If the great "listener of the people," Studs Terkel, was alive today, I'm not sure what he would think about our current situation. NO ONE WANTS TO WORK. Last night, I spoke with a dear friend who owns an excavating business in North Idaho. "Scott, I will pay my yard person $28 an hour to maintain the shop and general duties, but I can't find a taker." At our BBQ last Sunday, I heard the same lament over and over: "We can't find employees." When I moved back to Southeast Idaho, I brought my construction trailer and excellent company reputation with me, but I, too, couldn't find anyone to work construction. The carpenters who were worth their salt were working full-time and not interested. It has not changed. Those who want to work can pick and choose in this labor-starved environment.

In Terkel's book titled *Working*, he interviewed people across the country regarding their work and what it meant to them. Along with many of his other books, it became a bestseller. Terkel was serious in his pursuit. He wanted to understand work and why people engage in the jobs they do. One theme that came from all the interviews was this: Even if folks didn't like their current employment, they still wanted to work and feel good about themselves and their ability to put food on the table. Today, we took a Sunday drive. I personally saw six signs offering employment, and that was as I was watching the road. Who knows how many more I missed?

Restaurants locally are closing early or open fewer days of the week because of a labor shortage. The same is happening everywhere, including virtually every spectrum of the employment opportunity world. What does it mean? It means we have taken away incentives to work in many cases. As a lady friend of ours told us, "Why would you work here as a waitress when you can stay home and get paid three hundred dollars a week in unemployment from the government?" Yes, before you get yourself worked up, I understand that other factors can play a role. But often, her statement is true! And Government can't solve it, those gas bags can't do anything, it seems, at this point. Elected officials have little incentive to solve anything for the people. They are too busy shaping and endorsing their party and its stance to win that next precious election and keep their jobs secure. We elect them, and today's lack of a workforce can clearly be laid, in part, at their feet.

Yes, I remember my promise to not make my stories political. And besides, I simply do not have the cerebral acumen to explain the idiocy going on in Government.

Folks of my generation have a hard time understanding this lack of a work ethic. We grew up working. Working for enough money to go to the movie theater for a Saturday matinee and see Tarzan wrestle a lion. We worked for the new pair of fancy jeans or sneakers. We worked to buy our first car and keep it running so we could drive to college, get smart, and get a better job to build a future. In my family, the income was modest; it put a roof over our heads and food on the table. Extras we desired were up to us to provide for ourselves. I'm frustrated by this lack of personal integrity and pride in a job well done that's happening now.

One local potato processing plant has started advertising on TV a great starting wage with benefits and two dollars more per hour if you work the night shift. They are still without an adequate labor force. I have said this many times before: if it weren't for Hispanic labor in the fields, none of us would be eating. They do the hardest work that oft times family members of the farmer/rancher won't do. The trades like carpentry, plumbing, painting, and drywall cannot keep up with demand. No one wants to work in these labor-intensive fields anymore. But as my company plumber once said, "It will be a long time before your computer can fix your toilet."

And now for the good news. Our young lady, who comes in once a week to clean up after my slovenliness, pushed and pushed to get a better position after her current one looked like it would be eliminated. Her effort was Herculean, but she did it and it paid off. A new job with a bright light at the end of the tunnel called advancement. Another friend, who is fighting a difficult but not impossible illness, told my wife and me, "I was told I could go on disability. Why would I do that when I can still work?" She still edits a magazine daily for a firm in Boise. Sometimes from her bed, but she still keeps at it. She works for her family and her pride in being a productive individual who's not waiting for the next handout from Uncle Sam. This ethic moves me so deeply it could easily bring on tears, but I recover quickly as I think how proud I am of her and her desire to put out effort for that which she receives. A noble effort and an example for all of us to see and be humbled by. God Bless!

# Sport Shop Dreams

I spoke to my old car mechanic today about many things we both love and the past. He had just moved to the Upper Yaak River Valley in Montana, leaving the new massive influx of out-of-staters moving into Sandpoint, Idaho, behind. Jim has been a dear friend for lots of years and has kept our vehicles running beautifully over three decades.

Our discussions somehow always include a mutual, lovingly respected friend, Mr. Raiha. I always refer to Rauno (Ron) Raiha as Mr. Raiha and will continue to do so until the light fades forever. Mr. Raiha is special for a number of reasons, not the least of which is his mesmerizing smile that lights up the day. Whenever I entered the sanctum of the Pend Oreille Sports Shop, the first thing that captured my attention would be that grand smile. It was broad and welcoming, with true sincerity behind it. A Finlander with old-world manners and gentlemanly behavior, Mr. Raiha deserved the respect he was given. His sports shop was one of a kind because he knew it all intimately: rifles, fishing equipment, gunsmithing, camping, anything to do with the outdoors, and he gave advice that was sound and real. Not the palaver the outdoor stores of today offer, with their 57 isles of outdoor non-essential junk. From firearm calibers to lures and trout flies, his knowledge was encyclopedic.

Mr. Raiha sold me some wonderful old firearms. An original Sharps rifle and a vintage European shotgun, to mention two of the best. In fact, he told one employee, "When Scott comes and sees it on the wall, he will inquire about it."

Most of his unusual items caught my eye upon entry. My wife was not the sports shop type, but she loved going into his store. As I mentioned, he knew about everything, including her knitting projects, which he often commented on. Mr. Raiha had a special section for pipe tobaccos. This part of the store was a treat for the olfactory senses. It smelled so good I would sit at the end of the aisle while I scanned the wall for new arrivals. I have a balaclava pullover face mask in my outdoor pack that, to this day, retains that smell from being located on a store shelf near the pipe fillers. Sadly, ever so sadly, Mr. Raiha had to close the shop when a big box junk store with sporting goods moved in less than a quarter of a mile away. He gave me the inside story: "I can't buy my products for as cheap as they sell them; I don't have the huge quantity buying power they enjoy."

The last day, after the auction, I went in for the smell and heartbreak of one last visit. I asked Mr. Raiha if he had a leftover item I could buy to remember the shop by. He said, "You can buy nothing," then handed me a framed certificate that reads: "Zeiss Sports Optics Master Dealer, Pend Oreille Shop." It provides me with untold memories of a time gone by we shall not see again. I must mention, Mr. Raiha and his wife, with their old world responsibility attitude, raised three of the most remarkable, accomplished children to ever come from Bonner County.

Let's backtrack a bit now. The first love of my life in sport shops was Pocatello Hardware and Canvas. I have written about this mecca of wonderments before, buying everything 'outdoors' I could afford, even Mother's Christmas presents, which she accepted without hesitation or questioning my boyhood wisdom. In the basement of this hallowed building was Andy's Canvas Shop, where Dad ordered his custom wall tent, and every month on payday, he went in to put more money down toward its creation. The tent came, but the store closed sometime in the '60s.

Just down Main Street on the opposite side was a young man's dream, Freddy's Sport Shop. My parents told me not to go to Freddy's, my first and only year at Pocatello High, because it had a "tough image." Freddy's had a pool hall in the back where teen boys smoked! Heaven forbid, it was my first stop at lunch hour in high school. Only a block away from campus, we actually bought military surplus rifles and stored them in our school lockers until the end of the day. Imagine that today! Freddy's was the beginning of my Pool Career. My parents weren't impressed, nor were my counselors in high school nor were those in my first year of college.

Freddy's became Lee Akins Sports Shop after a time, and Lee Akins became a Pocatello landmark. I have so many items from there I could open my own sporting goods store. Lee was a longtime friend. I missed him when I moved away but would go see him when home for a visit. My nephew informed me when Lee died, and the next summer I went into the store to find his son carrying on the legacy. Alas, not long after, the son was killed in a motorcycle accident, and Lee Akins Sport Shop closed for good.

I leave you with a photo of the Zeiss certificate Mr. Raiha gave me. It will have a proud place in the sporting section of our house for as long as I am extant. It reminds me of happy days afield, beloved friends, some over the great divide now, and chatting with coffee in hand about the "big one just caught on the lake."

Photo: Zeiss Certificate.

# Under the Big Top

Pocatello, Idaho, is first and foremost in history, a railroad town. As such, a boy like me was treated to events not likely to happen in other locales in the West. Some towns lacked a railroad siding for special event trains like the circus. Circus caravans of train cars came every summer to our burg and were the peak of excitement for kids in the 1950s.

Two locations stand out in my mind as circus setups. One was on South Arthur, where it turns into Bannock Highway, the other on South 5$^{th}$ Avenue just past the old city cemetery. Bannock Highway runs along the railroad track for a mile before it crosses the Portneuf River, at the south end of Pocatello. It was here that the Ringling Brothers-Barnum and Bailey Circus, the Greatest Show on Earth, opened its tent flaps. This spectacular extravaganza disembarked from train cars and set up about 25 yards from the tracks.

When the circus came to town, my brothers headed to the setup point and worked as local "roustabouts." Their job was to help in any way needed, setting up the big top tents and carny booths. Mother would drive me out in the old Chevy to watch the elephants walk down their wooden railroad car ramps onto the siding and from there down into the field where they would pull up the big top tents, with massive ropes strapped to their shoulder harnesses. It was a wondrous sight that I remember vividly. My brothers worked all day moving and hauling, cleaning and washing gear. At the end of the day, their pay was two dollars and tickets to the circus, including one for me. My god, was I lucky!! Most of these circuses belonged to the 7 Ringling Brothers who bought out P.T. Barnum in 1907, formally uniting the two circuses in 1919.

The South 5th set-up was a bit trickier, as the elephants and cages had to be moved about half a mile to the site. The elephants walked along, pulling some of the lion enclosures on original hand-carved circus wagons from the early 1920s.

My brothers and sister indulged me and made sure I had spending money for popcorn and cotton candy. The arena master set me up right by the big rings that the animals and trapeze acts performed in.

Halliwell Baseball Park in Pocatello held the games for our Pioneer League team and also housed many other events because of grandstand seating. In the late 1950s, the Clyde Beatty Circus came to the park with great fanfare. My anticipation for this circus cannot be overstated! I scrimped and saved every penny I could from my various jobs, like shining my brother's Oxford shoes almost daily so they could work at a famous local railroad hotel. This grand establishment required dress-up attire.

Clyde Beatty, the Lion Tamer, held us spellbound as boys. We had seen him on newsreels at the theater before the Saturday matinee. Beatty trained lions, hippos, cougars, bears, and hyenas, among other animals. He was famous, to say the least, in a fascinated boy's eyes. The Beatty Circus at one point was so large it had thirty-five train cars. I sat in front of the grandstand on the lawn, right next to the cage that held Beatty and Nero the Lion. I was mesmerized as Beatty cracked his whip and used a chair to keep the lion at bay. Little did I know that Beatty had been mauled by Nero just the year before and was under a doctor's care for ten months! Once, on the Ed Sullivan Show, Beatty lost control of his act and Sullivan had to go out in the audience while the curtain came down, speaking to other celebrities and drawing attention away from the stage. The day I saw him, Mr. Beatty came out to the ring after the show, took his bows and, spying me in leg braces and using crutches, came over and autographed an 8x10 glossy photograph for me.

Imagine! I was the envy of every boy in town. The photo is missing from my collection of memorabilia. Perhaps someday it will reappear and I can be famous again.

The age of the Ringling Brothers Circus and big tops came to a close in 2017, after a run of more than a hundred and thirty years. Their demise was brought about by lack of public attendance, the Internet, and animal rights activists, the latter being their greatest foe. It has been said that circus animals were treated better than animals in zoos. I can't attest to this, but in April of this year, a call went out for a casting director to be hired to revive the travelling circus. Who knows, maybe someday Jumbo will again sit on a stool and lift his legs, in salute to an adoring audience of children and adults, who become kids again as they watch.

# A Teacher to Remember

"Whoop, thud!" The arrow sounded as it hit the back wall of the biology lab classroom. Mr. Whitlow had let sail another arrow while students worked on the test before them. Am I kidding? Not for a minute. Wayne Whitlow was a biology teacher of national renown, with a reputation for doing the most outlandish things a long-time educator could do. Whitlow signed on to the staff of Pocatello High School in 1927. By 1963, his retirement year, he was truly a legend around Idaho and the western states, not to be equaled in the student genius he turned out or wild behavior that would land him in jail today.

He was a time-locked character. Yes, he shot arrows down between the tall biology lab tables, using the wide aisle that separated each side row, progressing to the back wall of the room, while students read or worked on projects. And yes, he did murmur 'expletive deleted' language to rattlesnakes that didn't cooperate while he lost them on his long desk in front of the classroom.

On one occasion, a student came into the room with a message. Mr. Whitlow, engaged in a dissection, told the girl to read it out loud to him. The young lady proceeded with trepidation. The message related that a woman had a black widow spider in her window well, and she wondered if Mr. Whitlow wanted it. If not, what should she do with it? Without looking up from his project, Mr. Whitlow said, "Tell her to step on the SOB." The students subdued their laughter as he went on with his dissection presentation.

Eccentric? He was the real thing, biology and natural environments being his theater in life. Students were his prize each year, and he treasured their young minds open to his teachings. Biology students were not always happy being assigned to Mr. Whitlow's classes. He was a taskmaster who had each student make their own insect collection to be presented as a large part of their academic grade for the year. If you were in his class, working hard for your grade was not expected, it was insisted upon!

Mr. Whitlow had a hold on the school administration, who acknowledged his excellence. The 'powers that be' in the district offices recognized his genius in opening young minds and making them love what they were doing. His passion for biology was instilled in his class as part of his cranky demeanor, overridden by a quirky charm. My sister and brothers had Mr. Whitlow for high school biology. I did not, although I knew him my first year at Poky High.

To me, he was Mr. Whitlow, charter member of the Pocatello Field Archers Association. He gave me countless pointers on how to make long bows and shoot them. He taught great accuracy, as the Welsh Longbow men had been carrying out for centuries before. His ability with a bow was the stuff movies are made of. He knew legendary bow maker Howard Hill, perhaps the greatest bowman who ever lived. Hill made the shot in the Errol Flynn movie depicting Robin Hood splitting an arrow. This staggering shot by Hill left the movie makers standing around, mouths agape in disbelief. Luckily, I was able to procure a Howard Hill longbow later in life, a bow I own to this day.

As time wore on, Mr. Whitlow's fame grew as his indifferent nature became more pronounced. Professional associations across the nation counted him as one of their valued members, an unfailing academic contributor to their success. His taxidermy skills were superbly masterful, with some of his mounts ending up in the Smithsonian Museum, where they remain on display to this day.

My sister told of the time he dumped a bag of rattlesnakes out on the floor, between the closed fronted lab tables, to show students how they interacted. As one can imagine, this project could get out of hand, and it did. As the snakes crawled down the aisle between the tables some rounded the corners, sending students standing on the tabletops until Mr. Whitlow could get them all caught and accounted for. He turned to the students and said, "It's a good lesson for you all to learn. Count your rattlesnakes before you turn them loose." Apparently, he miscounted, as a janitor discovered later that day while mopping up after school. Just another Wayne Whitlow story to fill memory volumes recorded by former students, who still speak of him with reverence, or unprintable language, while describing antics like the rattlesnake roundup.

His biological knowledge was so vast he often lectured during the summers at universities around the West. At Pocatello High School, he supported all sorts of school activities, including making Native American headdresses for the school cheerleaders. The Boy Scouts bestowed high honors on Mr. Whitlow, as did other national leadership groups. Today, his former students are in the Idaho State Legislature, as well as a few having served in Congress. Universities have retired dozens of Mr. Whitlow's former students, some with their own national and international reputations and awards. In short, he taught, but moreover he gave students a chance and eagerness to learn and continue learning. A teacher worth revering!

Oh, by the way, come summer, the janitors at Poky High would remove his large, round, straw-stuffed archery target at the back of his biology lab, and re-plaster the old walls where holes were left by arrows that completely pierced the target. Years later, a long-serving janitor told me, "We smiled as we repaired the holes, saying to each other, 'he taught our kids how to think.'"

# Drugstore Cowboys

"Looks and dresses like a cowboy, but he has never done the work."

"A young man who loiters in public, like on corners or outside drugstore entries. Originally a reference to extras in Western films who would remain in costume off the set."

"Cowboy clothing purely for affectation or style."

Definitions of men my father had great disdain for and lamented their lack of class.

Being cowboy is back in style now. Not to the extent it had been before, like the late '70s and early '80s. Young men and women of citified upbringing were wearing high-dollar boots and outrageous cowboy hats with tight-fitting jeans.

I think the craze for the TV series *Yellowstone* has a great deal to do with it.

*Yellowstone* is one hellava series about the dilemmas of modern-day heritage ranching in an unforgiving and unsympathetic world. It does shine a light on how some big ranch outfits of today have to be in constant vigilance, in order to survive in this day and age of outrageous real estate values, values manipulated ever higher daily by propped-up markets that are bound to fail. It's an old cycle soon to be repeated; for some people it's a false surprise. It's been going this way for a long time, and as it does, it strips away at heritage ranching and farming operations, which barely survive from season to season working the land.

The land becomes the economy, an economy that is too tempting for children of the generations of the past to ignore. The land becomes so valuable that the great-grandchildren sell to the highest bidder. Nothing new here, but the TV series has brought home the greed and avarice in the real estate market, where large land holdings are in the scope of developers who care nothing for what happens to the land after the ink is dry on their contract. Is this wrong? I don't know, but I do know, it's what's happening at an alarming rate as the West is discovered once again.

Now the Drugstore Cowboys with boots have a new mantra for selling what they have no personal interest in except profit: LAND. As the profits increase for land sales, so do the tax bases when the land is revaluated after its last highest sale price. This cycle is going to force large land holding farmers and ranchers to regroup and figure out how they will survive in this new world of unexpected growth and everyone wanting their part of the wide-open spaces.

Buying a piece of wide-open space includes using water, and other resources growing ever more precious as the expansions move to where the sun sets. Never to be placed in the anti-growth league, I resign myself to the league of those who recognize what comes with this insane one-acre gentrified cowboy mentality that has overtaken the open skies. The land, and its natural resources that have sustained generations, is placed in great peril, never meant to be used sustaining great population influxes that do not understand its frailty and needed love, maintenance, and conscientious support.

When one sits in an ivory tower looking down, judgment should be withheld until the results of an action are in. I don't think we have time to wait to avert the coming serious growth dilemmas facing rural Idaho. Idaho is up for sale! The growth in Idaho is staggering, far more than we can handle without serious depletion of natural resources to the detriment of others. For those who lament, "To hell with the ranchers and farmers, they don't own the land." Yes, in many cases they do, and I suggest their perspective is better for looking at the future use of the land, rather than selling for a one-time quick profit and development.

Call them Drugstore Cowboys, salesmen, charlatans, or false dream weavers, the end result is the same. The land is divided, drawn and quartered, sectioned off into housing units or mini-ranchettes, never again to be a bound unit of natural grass growth or watershed storage. It is frightening to those who respect the land and its ability to sustain its fragile nature with a little help from its friends. Yes, growth is natural, but somehow this thought has been replaced with housing, motels, and apartments as better land use than historical ranching and farming. Therein lies the danger: not recognizing where land values lie in respect to preserving the lifestyle we have become so lazily accustomed to.

The plug has been pulled, and this is not my first rodeo in crying for help as Idaho's historic water table is slowly drained away. Not for cows and sheep, but for parks, golf courses, green spaces and miles of broad lawns that serve only a few yet consume millions of gallons of water to keep them green.

I bring this subject up as often as I can without sounding like a bad drumbeat, because the issue is serious. As I have said before, when you turn on the tap for a drink and the tap is dry, it's too late. I don't want to wait till the pail is empty before I figure out how to fill it again.

# Freedom Phil

Thanksgiving was an important holiday at my house when I was a child. It remains so in our house today. My dad was orphaned when he was twelve; his parents died within six months of each other. Mother lost her dad to the Spanish flu epidemic in early 1919. She was raised with six sisters by her mother, who never remarried. Both of them suffered hardships, and their family was everything to them, so we celebrated Thanksgiving with great enthusiasm.

Mother considered it the most important meal each year she prepared for her family. The cooking and baking started days before the event, and often twenty-five to thirty people crowded into their house on Willard Street in Pocatello for a feast that covered two tables, or more, with every festive food known for that occasion. It was heaven on earth, and both my parents took great pride in feeding the family and anyone else who stopped by.

We were taught to be thankful for all the blessings, hard work, and what our country gave us. We were also taught that sharing was equally as important as partaking. It was a simple time, and a simple set of lessons I hold dear to this day, which brings me to my topic: "Freedom Phil."

In 1994 I took delivery of a new '94 Dodge full-size van, with automatic doors and a grand lift which took me and my wheelchair up into this marvelous new rig. I could wheel down into the lowered floor modification, lock my wheelchair in with belts, and drive the van from my chair. Before this van I had to transfer from my chair to a van seat and then drive. This updated mode made life much easier.

Not long after I took the new van into my heart, I headed to Island Park and the Yellowstone country for my annual fall hunt and fishing trip with my nephew, Kent.

He and I proceeded to a creek near Kilgore and fished, talked, and reveled in the warm fall afternoon sunshine until an early dinner awaited us back at Ponds Lodge, where our wives would meet us. After we loaded into the van, I pushed the buttons to activate the door closers, and nothing happened. Knowing how to close the doors manually, we did so and then called my niece in Pocatello for advice on an access dealer who could set us up for an appointment for repair. Enter Phil.

"Here's a number for Phil at Freedom Access. He's a great guy, and I bet he can tell you how to fix the problem right there so you don't have to ruin your vacation coming down here." I drove us across the high plains out of Kilgore, while nephew Kent talked to Phil via cell phone and told him the symptoms and our faraway locale at the time. Phil patiently assessed the situation, then started telling Kent what to do and not do, and he was sure the problem could be solved with a few adjustments.

True it was. Kent worked on the door system outside our cabin and had it all working in an hour using the advice from Phil. Vacation saved. When I asked Phil later what I owed him, he said, "What? You owe me nothing; it was my pleasure." Almost an hour on the phone with painstaking guidance and no charge, I knew I needed to meet this guy.

The next summer, on a visit to Pocatello, I did meet Phil, had him adjust all my gadgets, and conversed with a truly dedicated man to those of us with special needs. When I left, he gave me some tires and wheelchair parts he no longer sold, again, no charge. This guy was a throwback to a time when people served with pride. Lots of years have passed, and I'm twenty-five minutes away from Phil now. I know a higher being brought this kind, funny, and good-hearted man into my life.

My beloved genius friend, Henry Hensheid, who motors around in the most incredible electric scooter, shares my love for Phil, as do all his clients. Wheelchair lifts, ramps, elevators, scooters, stair climbers, any gadget for the client who needs special accommodations to enjoy life to the fullest. We all know Phil is The Man.

His heart is as big as his humor, and we laugh with him. Traveling all over the near West, he does all installations and, to this day, runs a one-man shop. Phil started Freedom Access in 1995 and has not failed in service, warmth, or competence. If need be, he will come to our homes, troubleshoot, and fix problems associated with our special adaptive equipment.

Phil, we know you are having a well-deserved Thanksgiving getaway to Island Park with family. Enjoy your rest and holiday.

As we drove away the other day, after you finished my van lift service, Colleen said, "You should write a story about Phil." Here you have it.

Thank you from all your groupies, who march to the beat of a different drummer. Without you, getting down the path would be a lot tougher! Have an extra piece of pie, dear friend, and know you are appreciated and loved for keeping us going down life's good roads.

# P.O. Box K

Mrs. Burnham and Mrs. Dawson from the Elks Rehabilitation Hospital's physical therapy department brought me their box tops from various cereal companies, so I could order my ongoing prizes and model gifts from Kellogg's, Post, and other breakfast food giants. Mrs. Woods, the charge nurse, would have my room nurse tell me to come to the front desk because I had a package. The front desk was down a long hall of old barracks buildings, that had been the old Veterans Home in Boise. It then became the Elks Rehab Hospital for polio patients during the 1950s epidemic.

Hotter than the hubs of hell in the summer and cold in the winter, we managed with fans and those great old steam radiators for the chilly season. No one complained; it's what we had, and the staff was wonderful. I broke up my time between school classes and therapy, with weightlifting and courses in leather crafts and film developing. At this point in time, the idea of rehabilitation for those afflicted was pretty primitive. These classes helped me during long periods of cereal gift drought, waiting for those magic words: "Scott, go to the main desk, you have a package." Yes! THERE IS A GOD!

Mom was not a buyer of cereal in boxes; they were too expensive for our budget. Wheaties, Post Toasties, Cheerios, or Shredded Wheat were rare in our cabinet until my brothers moved out and the budget expanded. Aunts, neighbor ladies, and sometimes Mother would provide the needed two box tops, while I supplied 25 cents for my order going to: Kellogg's,

P.O. Box K, Battle Creek, Michigan. It was my weakness, and it's still around today.

Some of these items are collectible now, like my Hopalong Cassidy wallet, badge, crayon set, and photo of Hoppy and Topper, his faithful horse. The crayons are still like new and YES, I still have them, thanks to my father. Dad built me a huge toy box from scraps when I was little. After I moved out, he put all my old things in that toy box and padlocked it closed. When he and mother passed, it was truly like opening a treasure chest left by pirates.

Nephew Kent housed all my old, boxed collectibles after the family home was sold. Some of these treasures still await my first visual visit in almost 50 years. There are invaluable toys, and who knows how many of my cereal box treasures are waiting to be dusted off and pressed into service again!

Our postman, who walked the streets with his big leather bag slung over his shoulder, was a regular. As he would pass by on the other side of the street, he would holler over to me in the front yard, "Scotty, stay there, got a package for you." And my day would be made.

My brain raced with thoughts, "I wonder what it is this time?" I ordered so many items, so often, they arrived out of sequence. Perhaps it's my Dragnet badge and whistle, or my Superman rocket. Maybe my Lone Ranger badge, wooden 'silver' bullets, and mask? Or, my Century boats, all scale models. I have a Red Ryder bandana and Wheaties (breakfast of champions) baseball cards, along with a sign that says "Sugar Corn Pops, Shot with Sugar."

I took good care of all my toys and belongings; my father insisted on it. On his own from a very young age, he prized his possessions, respected and cared for them with love and the duty of ownership. This was instilled in his children, with firm admonishments if we failed to put something away after use. As a lesson well learned, I have much of these magical childhood memories in real version today. I still get joke toys for special occasions. Not long ago, I was given a D-8 Cat and a John Deere Backhoe.

Remembering the old adage "the only difference between men and boys is the size and cost of their toys," I try to keep myself in check today. When the TV ads come on with offers too good to be true, I'm full bore into this "once in a lifetime deal if you act now!" My wife laughs, and my nephew chokes back his amusement at his obtuse uncle's mind-set. What can I say?

My newest send-away was from my beloved, as she handed me a box that came in the mail. I looked at her and smiled sheepishly, while unbridled enthusiasm swept over me. WOW, a box from the postman. I'll be the envy of every boy in the neighborhood.

As I unwrapped my three new Tac-Lite flashlights, pen, bottle opener, whistle, and multiple other functions, my heart was glad—1955 all over again. Remember, "Order in the next ten minutes and mention this code. operators are standing by!"

# World Series Flu

A lesser-known phenomenon in the world of medicine comes only once a year, thank goodness. Coincidentally, it's around the end of the regular baseball season, after the pennant races have been decided and two teams are headed for the greatest of all sports tournaments, the World Series. It is strange that this illness is only prevalent around the end of September through the 15th or so of October. It can come on without a fever but often is associated with slight abdominal pains that can increase in severity as the final game approaches.

I thought of this malady the past couple of days, as my tummy has been out of sorts. But nothing as bad as the final day of the World Series, especially if the New York Yankees are playing. Our family physician, Doctor Wigle (pronounced Wygle), would ask my mother over the phone, "What are his symptoms, and what game of the Series is it?" After her filling in my recent medical dilemma, he would say, "Give him some tea with honey in it, a piece of toast, and make him rest. I'm sure it's the World Series flu. Call me in the morning if anything changes. My feeling is, he'll probably be better after the last inning." And, by golly, after the last pitch my recovery was miraculous! I would even, on occasion, want to go out and play catch with friends.

It was perfect… EXCEPT for Mother. If I stayed in bed, there was to be no bedside radio, just rest and regular trips to the bathroom to ensure the vermin were expelled from my body. The woman was a steadfast taskmaster. What difference would it make if, by chance, I turned on the radio and the

World Series happened to be on? But, "No, you are ill, and I don't want to chance it getting worse." Many years later, when I figured out the wily ways of mothers, I realized I'd been had!

As some of you have read in past stories, I sent for every prize advertised on a cereal box. In so doing, I received a dandy little crystal radio that looked like Sputnik, the Russian orbital satellite. The radio had a tiny earphone, so one could hear without sound being emitted to the room. To activate the receiver, you pulled the little silver antennae up and down until a good radio signal was found. It was a slow process. If the antennae were moved even slightly, the sound was gone.

Mother knew I had the radio, so when I heard her coming down the hall, I jerked the ear plug out of my ear and stuffed it under my pillow. That was how I beat the overlord that was my mother and listened to the Series! Did I fool her? Not for a minute! One afternoon, when afflicted with the 'Series' flu, she reached under my pillow to fluff it up and pulled out the radio. Looking shocked, I blurted out, "Boy, how did that get there?" She would say to my feigned surprise, "Remember, I have eyes in the back of my head and ears in every room." I was sure this was God's way of punishing boys who cheated and listened to the World Series when they were near death, waiting for the next stomach convulsion caused by the opposing team hitting a home run.

After the Series was over, Mrs. Cox, the doctor's office nurse, would call Mom and ask about my discomfort. Mother assured her I had recovered with amazing aplomb, to which Mrs. Cox would say, "It's a miracle how that works when the World Series is over!"

On the bright Monday, October 8, 1956, the world stood still waiting for the last breathless pitches of Don Larsen, the New York Yankee hurler. I had moved up to a Zenith transistor radio by then, listening in the back of the school bus with an earphone, I screamed out, scaring the other kids and causing Mr. Furrnet, the bus driver, to confiscate my radio. It mattered little, Don Larsen had just made World Series history, by throwing 97 pitches, pitching a perfect game and entering the record books!

Don Larsen moved to Hayden Lake, Idaho, in his later years. I had lived there in my early career in the north woods. Though I had two chances to hear him speak and meet him, the baseball gods did not smile on me, facilitating this happening. I did jot him a note about hearing the final pitches, where I was, and what happened with my Zenith. Who knows if he received the note, or if he even read it, but that doesn't matter. I remember that day as though it was last week; it still makes me smile, and that's what counts. We need more true sports heroes, not the overinflated, overpaid narcissists that permeate today's sporting events.

Honor, integrity, and humility are now replaced by the shallow glorification of celebrity. Hopefully, the ghosts of Lou Gehrig, Jackie Robinson, Mickey Mantle, Yogi Berra, and Hank Aaron, along with Willie Mays, will smile down and bring a spiritual revival to baseball. Perhaps the revival will spread to all other healthy athletic competitions, regardless of the shape or size of the ball.

# A Week

As I drove up Bridge Street, heading for the Groveland Cemetery, I glanced to my left while still in downtown Blackfoot to see the old J.C. Penney store had completed its remodel. For three years, I meant to take a photo of the fading painted storefront sign above the entrance. Like so many things, time seems to move faster than we do.

Old signs painted on buildings have intrigued me for quite some time. Many truly are works of art. Some old buildings have held up very well, especially on the leeward side of bad weather. The thought of the signs and old buildings, often needing repair to go on, was especially poignant as we moved along in our caravan, with headlights and flashers on letting the world know we were honoring a past friend or loved one. Drivers on the side streets held fast as we passed in slow procession. The cemetery was clean and orderly, as cemeteries tend to be, on a small rise looking out over the grain and potato fields, shining bright in the autumn sun, with a slight breeze bringing the smell of the harvest to our noses. This was Linda's new home, and it was perfect.

Linda and I grew up together, cousins and friends who had so many good times in our priceless years netting minnows out of her ditch, or helping row rubber rafts out on Island Park Reservoir to catch the big one. We made cooking fires in her backyard field. I shot at a pan she held while swinging with my BB gun, until a BB struck her bare leg. The BB gun was confiscated, and I was in big trouble.

Funerals are filled with so many emotions for each of us. To me, this one was a salvation as her health had been compromised for years. Her husband, a saint on Earth if there ever was one, was by her side day and night, giving all the aid she might need at any given time. When I spoke during the time for comments from those in attendance, I praised her husband for all his noble efforts on her behalf. Afterwards, numerous people in the group thanked me for my remarks outlining his loyalty. Then, I thought of the word "loyalty" and my dear friend Lorenzo (an ex-priest) saying to me, "Without loyalty, you have nothing."

The best part of funerals is seeing old friends and relatives with whom you have lost touch. Often, this may be the last time before your number has reached the scoreboard and it's time to move on. My friend Roger describes it as "needing to catch the waiting train." I got to see Linda's two sisters; the older of the two was my dearest friend and supporter in our bib overall years. These two ladies are "Ladies" of the first order, as fine as they were in childhood, with only a few year lines moving across their still beautiful faces. The church lunch afterwards was filled with happiness of life and seeing each other once again. Not bad at all!

The rest of the week was filled with the usual stuff, until Saturday. On Saturday, we went to see Elisa (E.C. Stilson, newspaper columnist), our beloved friend, and her family. Colleen took her a loaf of her world famous banana bread, and Elisa gave us homemade brownies. I asked her with a grin if these were the kind of brownies that gave one the munchies. To hear her uproarious laugh was worth the query. Not only has Elisa had her difficulties this past year, but poor Mike, her great husband, broke his foot and had surgery to correct the issues.

The kids came out and told me about school as I thought about what a great family they are, and how unbelievable life can be with all its ups and downs and sideways movements, never giving the secret to what's coming next. It just comes, and we deal with it as best we can, and truthfully it is the test of our mettle, and our class shows in how we handle it. This family has class in spades.

Elisa recently gave us a painting she had created. Yesterday she posted her latest painting effort, and it's truly amazing, as amazing as her commitment to life, her family, and all those around her who she feels need her help, even in the time of her own trials. On top of her prolific writing, she still finds time to play her violin for others. I invite you to see her on YouTube at: E.C. Stillson plays for fellow patients and staff at Huntsman. I made her an antler necklace and had it blessed with a Native American prayer to hold as she launches into her next round of treatments in Salt Lake City.

Know we are all pulling for you, and praying in our personal ways, sweet angel. Godspeed.

# Cleanup and Trish

I feel like I am always batting cleanup on the roster for a baseball team. When I try to formulate an exact plan for my next story, my brain throws me a curveball, and I'm off batting in the opposite direction. This past week, I have been talking on the phone to my old friend and early editor at the *River Journal*, about a book she is working on.

Trish published the dandy little *River Journal* for years, wrote and edited it late into the night to see that the word of the people got out. I had some stories in this grand little magazine and was often in there as a rebuttal commentator. Trish would call me, eliciting my opinion on a variety of subjects. She knew how to bait me, and get me to react, giving my unabashed thoughts that were often at odds with the rest of her readers. Trish is a beloved friend and has had her own battle with serious illness over the last year. Thankfully, she is doing well and back to being a combination of the author Hunter S. Thompson and Gandhi. Her brain works faster than her typing and keeps her questioning everyone and everything.

Trish is a chronicler of life, present and past, which brings us to her latest query into an incident of the past. An unsolved murder in her long-distant family history. This is where I came in. One of my many oddities is firearms knowledge, types, historical usage, manufacture, and a bit of forensics based on calibers, shotgun bores, and armaments of the day. Besides, my sharing of information, while maybe not the best one could get, is priced right.

Her family murder mystery begins in the early 1880s, and I think she really is onto a good story. As we progressed in our discussion, between Sandpoint and my kitchen table now north of Blackfoot, I recognized what a favor she was doing for me. In thinking of firearms history, one is thinking of history in a time and place. I once wrote that firearm histories tell an incredible story of human development and progress. I also believe that if you want a good knowledge of the world, take a series of art or architectural history courses. Both are proofs of human intrigue, deceit, politics, creativity, and recognition.

After the first call, I started thinking of Trish and her remarkable child-rearing in tough circumstances. Basically, she did it on her own from a cabin heated with wood, caring for kids over long, hard winters while maintaining a foot in creativity, with her hometown magazine and writings. She did it all. Write, edit other writers, publish, and travel all over, distributing the magazine in a very rural area. It was not an easy task. Her sense of humor never left, nor was there any hint of despair when outsiders knew life was not treating her well. She plodded on against odds that were not favoring periodical news magazines and the printed word. The world of cyberspace news moved in with its faceless, wrinkleless, noiseless white light information, which truly lacked the personal touch of a newspaper folded back to complete a crossword puzzle. We have not gained from it! It reminds me of the old saying: "The telephone will never be a success."

Trish explored words as do I, words not often used in daily conversation, but important to maintain nevertheless. Churchill, Dylan Thomas, and other giants of the English language, like W.B. Yeats, had vocabularies in excess of 70,000 words, while the average active English student may use 20,000. We often use no more than 3000 words to communicate each day, with only 700 or so rounding out the normal range in some arenas.

Trish's opinions were the truth as she knew it. She did not lie or hint at another explanation when obvious realities were evident. In today's world, truth seems so elusive and abstract. Round is square, hot is cold, and truth seems more and more at odds with representational thought. Trish fought for truth to the end of her magazine's publication, and I admire her for it.

It is rare now for publications to seek, and more importantly, print, the truth, even if it is indelible before them. Like Trish, Ann Anthony, editor of the *Island Park News*, gives her writers the same respect. It is the most important task we have as citizens: seeking and demanding truth! A life worth living is a life worth being honest. And Trish, you were always honest even if I didn't agree with all your positions. I still admired your guts, putting yourself out there to suffer possible owliness from old grumps like me. I salute you, Ms. Gannon (my favorite salutation for her).

What you did for the public with the *River Journal* was hugely important. I am sure your current work with that notable Sandpoint publisher is equally as appreciated. Carry on!

# What's Right

For the past two or three years, I have been reading articles by a twit who writes for a major newspaper south of here, here being north of Blackfoot, in the farm country where the Hispanic farm workers are busy as bees in a blossoming cherry tree. Looking out to the field watching these hardworking people, I thought about a common denominator they all seem to have: love of family and children.

They seem to find joy in the face of hard labor and, in some cases, inequities. That brings me back to the twit. Actually, two twits with different names.

Both of these columnists appear in the Sunday only edition of the newspaper: thank God! Neither one of these characters has, as I can remember, written a positive column, or anything without a doom and gloom scenario! Why do I read them? So, I can do exactly as I am here-trying to understand their reasoning and dispelling the venom and regurgitated B.S. they spew.

We are sorely in need of original thought, not the same news item told over and over with a different voice. One of these characters was a year or so behind me in school. He was born with the proverbial silver spoon in his mouth. The other in this twinship is a perfect example of never leaving an institution of higher learning after graduating. They become lackeys in one supportive bureau or another. Rarely have they worked outside this safe arena my friend Tim calls "the public trough," in short, those that have jobs based on tax dollars the institution is awarded each year. Never having to face layoffs or dismissal without reason, these twits are carried well, entering the future with a safety net of guaranteed government retirement. But both of these men have nothing good to say about any life benefits they have received, as far as I can tell, and continue on the 'everything is wrong' bandwagon. This attitude annoys me no end!

I ask, "What's right?" In my head, it becomes overwhelming when I hear repeatedly, from many quarters now, the litany of how bad everything is. I wrote a letter to the editors of the newspaper carrying their articles a couple of years ago, rebutting one fellow's argument. Apparently, the paper liked the letter. Though it was very short, they reprinted it several times.

Some types who work in the news media today will view a kitten pulling apart a ball of yarn and say, "Kitten destroys priceless woven fabric art globe. Kittens need to be banned!"

I know it's silly, but so much is! Yes, we, the world, the universe (I suspect) have problems. But I feel identifying the same issue three thousand times in a slightly different way still lacks an answer for solving the difficulty. Dentists would offer their patients an answer to eliminate a bad tooth. That's all I want of media types when I ask, "What answers do you have?" Give me an idea for a solution, a plug for the leaking dyke, new asphalt, how to achieve cleaner sand boxes. Anything, but suggest a solution to the problem that's clearly outlined. Of course, this rarely happens because they do not have a solution, or they're afraid to publish it for fear of retribution.

In this year's primary election process, I have witnessed the worst of the worst in TV and newspaper advertisements for candidates. NOT ONE CANDIDATE spoke of solutions! They readdressed the problems we are all aware of, much the same as the newspaper columnists.

What's right to me is watching the field workers plant, seeing their camaraderie and mutual support. Laughter fills the air as they pass our north fence, moving pipe or sprinkler heads time and time again. It's right that I love seeing nature in all its forms and curiosities. It is right that I send letters to editors, but only if I can suggest credible solutions to troubling matters at hand.

We have so much that is right! We do live in the land of milk and honey, compared to much of the rest of the world. Our social insecurity surprises me. Quasi-intellectual snobbery and narcissism have reached new heights, all while awaiting their ivory tower legs being chopped off.

Honor and dignity seem sadly lacking in visual reportage and print. Old concepts? Perhaps, but both words are woefully needed as part of the public fabric and discourse.

If I were to address the two twits I spoke of, my first question would be, "Gentlemen, what is right in our lives? Please answer that before you proceed to describe all that's wrong. We need an enlightenment." The guy who answered with, "That kitten was so damned cute" would get my attention, readership and, in appropriate instances, my vote.

# T. Bird

Coffee was cooling and spuds being peeled as my nephew's son, Chris, picked up his fishing pole and headed up Sawmill Creek. No words said, he sauntered off into the wilds of Idaho's eastern mountain Lemhi Range. At ten or so, he understood keeping an eye out for things that could eat ya, bite ya, or stab ya, returning a quarter hour later with a mess of brookies, rounding out breakfast in that rare mountain air. Tim grinned, saying, "That's the kind of kid to have."

Later, we headed to the tiny crossroads store in Howe, Idaho. It was too damned hot to hunt the mule deer we were after. On the way down the valley, near the Little Lost River, the dusty, rough trail abruptly became a paved stretch. I commented with Tim replying, "See that driveway? It belonged to a former County Commissioner who had the road paved to his ranch." I smiled, having seen the same thing in North Idaho after years living there and following local politics.

Starting the day, I met him, Tim Bird taught me more about politics than any university could. He knew politics and how to get things done better than anyone I ever met. Tim was a leader in Herndon's gubernatorial campaign before the campaign ended in a plane crash. He involved me in the circles of Idaho's legendary Senator Frank Church, Governor Andrus, and future Governor John Evans. These introductions lead to a conviction that change was possible if one tried. He also taught me politics can be the dirtiest business of all.

Let's drift back to my first meeting Tim in Pocatello. In 1974, I interviewed for a special project the government was sponsoring, called S.S.I. Alert. The goal was to locate citizens who had never worked due to being aged, blind or disabled and lacking any income. Sponsored in Pocatello by the Red Cross, the scope covered sixteen Eastern Idaho counties. As I left, a man I had seen in the group of interviewers met me outside the door and said, "Let's go down the street and get a cup of coffee."

Near the famed Bannock Hotel, we took up a table in the coffee shop. He was quiet as I sized him up, a not-too-tall man with the most beautiful silver hair I had ever seen. Cowboy boots and western outfit true to the image, most of all I remember the cloak over his shoulders, Sherlock Holmes style, that worked perfectly with the visage. Ladies would, and did, call him handsome. Asking about my life, I filled him in as best I could on the spur of the moment. He sat silent. Later, I learned from the director of the Red Cross that "the cowboy representative from the Idaho Office on Aging convinced her that I was the man for the job." Tim saw me, the man, in spite of the wheelchair.

Over the next twenty years, we traveled countless roads together as he, and sometimes his son Brett, would join nephew Kent and me in Island Park for our annual fall hunting and fishing trips. This was Tim's old stomping grounds, having grown up in view of the Tetons, riding racehorses and cowboying the area in youth. His hunting stories in Island Park surrounds were enthralling, picketing his horses in the woods near his favorite Phillips Lodge. I have a photo from his rodeo announcing days at the great Island Park Rodeo.

Beyond politics, he taught me horses. I loved horses and spent time with horsemen who talked a good line but most often repeated common training mantras. Tim knew horses! He learned from old masters, like crippled-up racehorse trainer

Ralph Garner. He rode Ralph's horses and cowboyed. Fred Jackson once told me a story of him and Tim roping a bobcat out in the hills of Kilgore when they were wild young hombres.

Tim came to Sandpoint for a visit one October while his wife attended a conference in Spokane. At the draft horse show, we met my beloved southeast Idaho shirt tail kin Wells Barney. Wells was the dean of western draft horsemen. I related a story that a Sandpoint real estate agent, erstwhile draft horse trainer, had spewed. Hearing that story, Tim told a group, "Wells Barney knew more about horses in his crib than that knot head will ever know."

Where to start and end in this hardest part of Tim stories. He and his wife, Colleen, saved my bacon countless times when I would step on the wrong politician's foot or hopeless bureaucrat's ego. Colleen promoted me for two gubernatorial appointments on State Advisory boards.

At a conference in Lewiston long ago, I picked Tim up to go to the college for the day. He looked at me and said, "Go east, we're going to pick up Charlie Taylor (beloved Nez Perce friend and elder) and go look at Nez Perce horses."

Oh, before I forget, my wife found the Ray Lum book I have spoken about in what she called "plain sight." Opening the book, a letter from Tim dropped out. In it were words of beautiful memories, and tears welled up. His last line was, "Like Ray Lum, I need my speedometer turned back."

Speaking at his funeral, I asked God to give him a horse. For years I tied feathers to his headstone near Boise on my way south, and I still build a fall fire for him in Island Park as promised, when I can. Tim, I will always hold you and your words about life and horses close to my heart and wish you good rides on a broken-in saddle. Your words sound in my ears:

"Nothing prettier than the sun going down over a horse's back."

# America's Longest Main Street

Dad rarely engaged the gears without a grinding sound, downshifting our 6-cylinder, 3-speed, '49 Chevy as we made the long climb from Warm River up to the flats leading past Mesa Falls on old Highway 47. As a young lad, that's how we accessed Island Park and Yellowstone. My father (and his siblings) were unwittingly bad drivers! Mother and I gripped door handles, ready to bail, in case he wandered too far off the road onto the shoulder, which would have plummeted our car into Warm River at the bottom of the grade. Somehow, we made those trips, not because of Dad, but drivers gave him the road, which was a wise move on their part. The two of us would eventually get the blood back in our white hands after having held on so tightly.

My father spent a great part of his early life in the Idaho Teton Basin and Island Park, working wherever he could, in the woods, road building, or on a haying crew. If it was hard labor, he was your man. Big trucks suited Dad better than cars. When my parents finally acquired a new car with a V8 engine, Mother called him Mario Andretti because he would quickly accelerate from stop light to stop light. Most of his early life was spent driving teams of horses and Model T Fords. For years, we didn't own a car. Dad rode his bike or walked to the railroad yards, Mother and I rode the city bus to go shopping.

The Mesa Falls Scenic Highway, as it is now called, was beyond beautiful. It snaked through woods coming out on meadows, marshes, and sagebrush flats. Open areas that somewhere along the way would reveal moose, mule deer, antelope, elk, and often bears, including grizzly. In those days traffic was not the issue that it has become today, with vastly differing opinions about the roadway's future.

When the new pass from Ashton, that rose more directly from the valley floor, was finally finished, it made Island Park access a lot easier and quicker. But there lies the kicker. Should it be made into a four-lane highway through most of Island Park to where it intersects State Highway 87? I have followed the proposals made by the Idaho Transportation Department and old engineering studies religiously. I offer the following:

After Island Park incorporated, it became known as America's Longest Main Street. The city limits are narrowly strung along Highway 20 for 36.8 miles, basically from Valley View to Last Chance. Back in the day, this was done to afford liquor licenses to local bar and lodge establishments. Now, that same stretch of road is world famous for its scenic beauty, along wetlands that rival Alaska muskeg, and tree-lined miles that take one to Yellowstone's western gate. When a traveler breaks from the woods after passing the old Island Park Lodge, the flats appear with vistas of divine natural landscape flowing to Henry's Lake and West Yellowstone. "Breathtaking" is inadequate for describing its splendor. To me, it's as close to heaven as one can get without bumping into the pearly gates.

This beautiful highway has proposals now being made that would, in the future, bring a four-lane limited access highway across wetlands and area geothermal features that must not be lost! The four-lane consideration is obtuse, obscene, and against rational ideas offered as alternatives to this destruction. Destruction that cannot be reversed upon completion. Many damaging things can be outlined regarding a four-lane highway in Island Park, not the least of which is dividing America's

Longest Main Street. If completed, access to homes, ranches, shops, and recreational areas would be diminished twenty-fold.

In other words, driving miles of frontage roads would be needed before reaching access points to Highway 20. A four-lane highway would severely limit ease of movement to Coffee Pot Rapids, Harriman State Park, and countless other natural attractions, along with business venues and residences that line the roadway on both sides. If not a four-lane, then what?

The existing highway traffic studies are woefully lacking in updated information and statistical data regarding this glorious drive. Outdated and speculative statistics are being considered by the Idaho Transportation Department and its board of directors, who ultimately make the final decision. Without question, the majority of native dwellers, businesses, and recreationists are adamantly against a four-lane freeway-type roadbed.

Alternative answers for the future of Highway 20 have been outlined by knowledgeable, concerned citizens, offering sound, safe, and intensely examined upgrades.

Locals, county residents, and frequent travelers from throughout the West have all offered opinions and options to a four-lane behemoth and its designated mates: high-woven wire fences along each side of the road, giving way to occasional and randomly spaced wildlife overpasses.

It need not be! Simpler, more cost-effective, and less impactful solutions exist, including increasing the number of passing lanes, creating wider shoulders in some areas for emergency pull-offs, and budgeting more state/county law enforcement patrols.

The traffic studies being used are old and inadequate, primarily addressing peak seasonal travel during the summer.

For most of the year, this highway has far less use when kids are back in school, vacation travel is over, and winter temps move in.

The Island Park caldera is a wondrous place on our Earth, created by the massive collapse of Yellowstone's ancient volcanic activity. It cannot, it must not, be lost to silly bureaucratic, outdated wrong-thinking planning. Planning that has little merit for anyone but highway contractors and their ilk, who will promote the design process for economic advantage alone. We must save this idyllic, iconic drive, with reasonable adaptations. It can be done by making ongoing cost-conscious, simple upgrades. Doing so will ensure a drive-through paradise for the coming generations. Countless visitors will see what existed in the beginning of recorded time, and what still remains, mindfully altered with conscious reverence for all to enjoy.

# 'Dubby'

On Tuesdays, early in my student career at Idaho State University, I would venture to the Reed Gymnasium basement on campus and shoot at the ROTC range. It never failed when Dubby would see me, he asked about my dad. Dad boxed in the Marines in the early 1920s. That, and an old Northwest boxing champ Dad worked with, were the connection. A connection I never really appreciated until much later in life. As I have written before, into his eighties, my father could grab a fly out of the air. He had the fastest hand movements I personally have ever witnessed. It came from boxing! Sugar Ray Leonard, with his lightning hands, could have learned from Dad.

'Dubby' was Milton 'Dubby' Holt, legendary athletic coach and director of the athletic programs at ISU. He was a field and track champion as well as an all-star football player, still retaining the punt return record of 88 yards at ISU.

Bill Hall, Idaho's dean of newspaper journalists, wrote in the *Lewiston Tribune* upon Dubby's death in 2007: "He coached swimming with championship teams and couldn't swim. He coached championship boxing teams and didn't box."

That was the integral part of Dubby, it took many years and distance for me to appreciate. His acute intelligence led him to read everything he could consume on a topic and turn it into magic. His magic guided him to coach boxing at the Melbourne Olympics in 1956. *Sports Illustrated* listed him as one of the best collegiate coaches of all time. While at the Melbourne

Olympics, one of Dubby's fighters defeated future World Heavyweight Champion, Ingmar Johansson.

Long before I knew Skip Newton of Sandpoint, Idaho, my friend, Fred Kennedy, would say over coffee at our 4 o'clock Liars Club, "Skip Newton could have gone all the way if they hadn't dropped collegiate boxing at ISU." Yes, Skip was that good!

A Golden Glove and Inland Empire AAU champion, his college career and scholarship ended with college boxing's demise. Skip was given a football scholarship, but decided he needed to go home and find a paying job.

So many old Pugs, like Skip, are the quietest, most humble of men. They have nothing to prove. The ring gave them self-confidence and character in those days.

Dubby played a key role in Skip's life, and thousands of others. Helen, Skip's wife, said to me once, "Oh, my gosh, if I had a dollar for every Dubby story I've heard, I'd be a millionaire." Dubby was that kind of guy. His influence lives on to this day, in the covered Sports Dome at ISU that bore his name.

When Dubby proposed the originally named Mini Dome, there was only one other covered sports dome in the world, in Houston, Texas. The Mini Dome became the second. Much of the student body at ISU opposed the dome, as a waste of student fees and taxpayer dollars. Single-handedly, Dubby raised support. Now, it is believed the dome has generated more than a hundred times the original revenue it took to build it.

Today, the Holt Arena hosts countless events, from agriculture to car shows, rodeos to high school and college championships, across the broadest range of endeavors.

Currently, Holt Arena is undergoing a massive remodel and facelift to accommodate an even more eclectic, broad-based arrangement of events. It has become a tri-state mainstay for public gatherings.

I'll give you another side of Dubby, the common man side. After college, I took a job in Kingman, Arizona. While at the agency I worked for, I was assigned to help develop the senior citizen center concept before it became widely endorsed by the government. On two occasions when folks found out I had graduated from ISU, they would approach me asking if I knew Dubby Holt. Two that I recall had been janitors at the gym. Each day, when Dubby passed them, he would stop and tell them their job was the most important on campus and truly mean it. He loaned money to many struggling gym staff and helped them find reasonable housing. Dubby had the ear of the city fathers, bankers, and philanthropists, and he used it wisely. He was a modest man, with several championships in his personal belt from his time competing in the collegiate world.

I watched an Ali/Frazier fight on the big screen live at the dome soon after it opened. After the fight, which I scored much differently in my own book, I went to our local college pub and made the mistake of saying Ali was not the greatest heavyweight of all time, Rocky Marciano was. After the boos stopped, I pointed out that Joe Lewis, had he not suffered a brain injury, would have smoked em' all.

My old bus driver, Dale Trumbo, fought alongside Skip at ISU. I later scored some Smoker events in Coeur d' Alene for Dale, when he headed up the Idaho Boxing Commission. It was a thankless job that almost got me thrown into the lake, but it was exhilarating. I am an old-style boxing fan. When he was a teenage fighter, I predicted "Iron" Mike Tyson would become the youngest Heavyweight Champion of the World.

Dubby's style taught me well about observation. In 1999, Dubby was inducted into the Idaho Sports Hall of Fame. In 2007, that great Hall of Fame in the sky claimed him. Long ago, former Island Park mayor (and coach) Tom Jewel selected me to be student manager of Highland High School's championship wrestling team. Coach commented daily on lessons he had learned from Dubby. Later, he joined Dubby's coaching staff at ISU. As a true sports world giant, Dubby, you will always be a Heavyweight.

Photo: Skip Newton boxing trophies.

# Father Tim

Arriving a bit late to Eddy's wake and outdoor relaxed eulogy session, on a beautiful hill near the old Hope, Idaho, cemetery, my thoughts were on what a perfect day for Eddy's (Edwina) last hurrah. Her memory still fresh, and the hurt very real to all of us who loved her so. Sitting in the sun lost in thought, I heard my name called by Father Tim saying, "And now we'll hear from Scott Hancock." Taken totally by surprise, I pulled myself together and gave an impromptu remembrance, gathering thoughts from our times past, our moment of history together as best I could. Afterwards, I said to Father Tim, "I didn't know I was to speak." He said, "Neither did I. The idea just came to me seeing you in the audience." It was normal, from this incredibly normal priest.

My first encounter with Father Tim was in Hope when he pulled up while we were unloading a moving van, and said "Hi, my name is Father Tim, welcome to the neighborhood." The Mr. Rogers greeting made me smile. Tim was slight, with a cute little mustache and cap that looked like he played golf in the 1930s, and perhaps he did. He was to touch my life in countless ways, as he did for Catholics and anyone he came in contact with. He loved unconditionally, with a heart that gave and gave to all that wanted his shared giving and forgiveness. He was as true a representative of God's council as I have ever met on Earth. He was real!

Timothy John O'Donovan was proud of his Irish heritage. Cute as a leprechaun, he carried it well in his service to mankind. Serving many parishes, he was semi-retired when

I met him, but still roaming the north counties, as he was needed to fill in when other priests were called away from their flocks. His service to the little Clark Fork, Idaho, parish was ongoing.

Tim had a nature that made him loved by all, including agnostics and atheists. His kind demeanor told who he was before you knew he was a priest. Tim's retirement day-to-day dress wear kept his priest identity from most who encountered him. Humble in all ways, he drew no attention to himself. His mission was one he took very seriously, a calling he proved time and time again in his unfailing care and concern for others.

Called from his bed untold times to give Last Rites, to those who requested, they wanted only, Father Tim. Friends of mine in law enforcement spoke of the counseling Tim gave to the incarcerated, and those that had endured family tragedy, regardless of religious affiliation, as his own frailty in his retirement progressed.

Once at Della Santina's Italian Restaurant in Sonoma, California, Tim was ensconced when my wife and I arrived for lunch seated with my Sandpoint friends Jim and Pam Lippi's California cousins. The Lippi's Ivano's Italian Restaurant in Sandpoint, Idaho, was directly influenced by Jim's cousins in Sonoma. Father Tim was a part of both these families who adored, cared for and guarded him carefully to the last day of his time on Earth.

My friend Jim Lippi hosted my 55$^{th}$ birthday dinner at Ivano's, with nearly ninety people in attendance. Jim prepared moose roasts which I provided, in Tuscan style. To say it was outrageously good would be correct. At this gathering, I reversed the surprise request to speak to Father Tim. Without notice I asked Tim, as he visited with friends, to bless our food. Let me point out, some he visited with were hardened nonbelievers. Tim had them all spellbound, lowering their heads for his prayer of peace and goodwill for all. When the group left, some of the most outspoken nonbelievers came to me and thanked me for having Tim do a prayer.

To a person, Tim had touched them, or someone they knew, in a positive, personal way. He was truly widely loved by all who knew him!

Father Tim was made a Monseigneur by the Catholic Church in his last years, an occasion he called to ask my wife and I to attend. We attended many celebrations of Tim's life and his service to the church.

I once told Tim my history of working with nuns and priests, especially in working with Native American tribes. I told him of Father Patrick Duggan, whose brogue was so thick one had to lean in to understand what he was saying, Father Lorenzo, who Tim knew well, and Father Scarcello (lifelong farmer), who, as Tim said, "often came into the church with cow pies on his boots." I once told Tim my favorite Catholic joke, that had been told to me by Father Scarcello, while some very pious ladies sat shocked nearby. They were horrified as Tim laughed, and when I told him Scarcello had told me the joke, he laughed louder!

Tim was, as is said of another great theologian, a man for all seasons. His quiet, calm, and soft, assuring voice was a gift. We spoke often on the phone just before he left this earth. In one evening call he said to me, "My friend, it has been my blessing to know you." My eyes grew damp as I thought of the wonderful things he had done for me and others, unselfishly with love. Forever rest in the arms of the Lord, old friend, may others you touched emulate your faith, honor, and unfailing goodness.

L. Scott Hancock

# Auntie Pat

A year or so ago, I watched a TV documentary about an astonishing lady in Napa Valley, California, and her decades dedicated to home delivered meals for in-home senior citizens. It turns out, the documentary has been played in countless areas of California and other states. The ride-along video with Auntie Pat, as she is known affectionately, was in the same 1993 Volvo station wagon that the interviewer had ridden in ten years before while making a similar documentary. He asked if it was the same car and Pat assured him it was and would remain so as long as she delivered meals.

The car is as legendary as Pat Wartenweiler. Ordered special because she "wasn't too lazy to roll windows up and down," it is her personae, along with her great British accent and smile, a combination of Julie Andrews' charm and Margaret Thatcher's iron-willed determination. In the annals of volunteerism, Pat must rank at the top, her home-delivered meal career topping 40 years.

When she is rarely absent, a substitute is arranged ahead of time, and when she goes on trips abroad with her husband, Dr. Franz Wartenweiler, she sends postcards to all of her shut-ins. She forgets no one on her route, and when holidays roll around, she bakes them her English tasties or provides them with homemade jams or jellies. They are her family, and she theirs. Her devotion has helped save at least one senior in dire straits.

A fun note here is that countless young people approach her when she parks her car in store shopping lots to ask if she would sell her Volvo. Her answer is politely the same: "No, it will die with me." This past Christmas, she told me over the phone, "I got a new car for Christmas." I was dumbfounded until she explained her husband, Dr. Franz, had the car completely refurbished, with detailing inside and out.

Pat's route of delivery around the gorgeous Napa Valley takes her to a variety of valley vistas and neighborhoods. Her clients wait patiently each day, not just for the meal, but for an encouraging word from Pat. She is always optimistic and outspokenly honest in help. She a slight lady, thin and fit, who walks daily and takes her dogs for jaunts in the English tradition. In the past, she has taken in the animals of departed senior friends at their request, even a chicken that showed up at one senior's house. She gave the chicken to a neighbor but took its first egg back to the senior citizen!

Pat is married to my deceased wife's brother, Dr. Franz Wartenweiler, and has been for many long years, beginning shortly after they met shipboard coming from England. Pat and friend, Jennifer, had jobs in New York, but continued on to California, hitching a ride with Franz and a friend. And the rest fell into place. After marriage, the couple lived in Switzerland, Australia, and other locales, pursuing careers until Franz settled on chiropractic medicine. His office was located in St. Helena, California, where his reputation gained great respect. Chances are good if you are drinking a Napa Valley wine from a major vintner, Dr. Franz has attended to one of the family members.

Raising three successful daughters while doing her volunteer work, Pat managed her special pets in proper fashion as well. Currently she has rescue donkeys that are blessed to have her. She champions the cause of opening vineyards to animals during range fires. Vineyards are watered and remain lush and could serve as a safe haven during the ravages of Napa Valley fires.

Both Wartenweilers have been community standard-bearers for volunteer support. Franz rose to celebrated ranks in Rotary International, even travelling to Vietnam to oversee village water restoration projects.

A couple of years ago, they visited us here in Blackfoot. Pat brought her own tea for tea time, and tea biscuits as well. She's the real deal, and God, I love her for it. Each morning after a brisk walk, she would return to say, "This is my kind of countryside," although at one point she did have to step off the road, to give way to a passing potato truck. Early on, learning of my life's study of Churchill, Pat shared a photo of her father and Winston together.

And now a few points of clarification. Yes, the family has other vehicles besides the Volvo. And yes, she has the wherewithal to purchase another Volvo, but "What's the point? This one works very well and I love it." Her great British sense of thrift and economy does not play to ostentatious behavior.

And lastly, here's a smile maker. Aunt Pat is eighty-five, older than most of her clients and still going strong, with no end in sight! As Churchill would say," Pat, here we are, CARRY ON!"

# Last Chance

I felt the smile cross my face as the young man walked to the door and out, eventually ending up in the North Fork of the Snake, pitching a fly to a wary trout in wait for its next flying bug. His image was one straight off the cover of Fly Fisherman or Orvis catalogues, or a photo of any river in the West with a fly caster plying the waters. Photogenic and created by the wardrobe department of a major publication, he was perfect against the rainy sky and cold blasts coming down from Yellowstone. As he crossed the lawn in front of my window, while waiting for a burger at the Trout Hunter Lodge, his ensemble was laid out according to the latest in fly fisher fashion. Hip waders color-coded to his raincoat, color-coded to his hat, with the ubiquitous dip net draped tautly across his back to be pulled into action at a moment's notice. And I haven't mentioned the gorgeous fly rod and reel he carried. It alone was pricier than many good used cars!

At the same time, somewhere in the distance, I heard an earth disturbance. I sat apprehensive, until I realized it was Dad rolling over in his grave with laughter at the sight before me! At the very same spot, the young man waded out into the river, I had seen my dad do the same countless times, with his old Orvis bamboo rod, in his work pants, barefoot or with old tennis shoes he owned for just such an occasion. How he stood the cold waters for as long as he did each trip is beyond me, but he did and often waded a quarter mile downstream before coming ashore to warm his feet. His only other accoutrements were the old wood landing net that floated behind him, attached to his waist with bailer twine, and the beautiful leather fly book with its felted pages, loaded with flies from my Uncle Cece's tying vise or from Frank, his friend, who owned the cabins and gas station in Last Chance, Idaho. Last Chance is a burg, or a wide spot in the road, on that "longest main street in America," claimed by the Island Park powers that be. We stayed at Frank's cabins rarely; tent camping was cheaper, but Frank often gave Dad a deal so the family slept in the warmth of a wood stove-heated cabin on those chilly fall days.

The cabins are still there but have fallen into disrepair. And the area around them, sadly, is in need of attention. I am not sure why this remains the case in this era of outside money buying, and in my book, ruining the once beautiful ambience called nature. While Dad waded the river, Mother would watch as I fished from the bank in that shallow rippled stretch with fly rod, casting stone flies, or, when that failed, my South Bend spinning rod, tossing Colorado spinners until some uninterested trout had a change of heart.

For those who have read my stories, you recognize my IP memories. Some of my finest times in life have been spent within a stone's throw of Yellowstone. Even when I lived in North Idaho I came home in the summer or a week in the fall, for fishing and hunting in that magic country.

The bison burgers arrived as my nephew Kent, with a French fry closing in on his lips, said, "Remember the time we remodeled tire chains on that old cabin table, to fit the small wheels on your Datsun station wagon?" Yes, I remembered. We were at one of Frank's cabins, arriving early before my family came up to start the next morning, the opening day of the elk season. We fixed the chains and installed them, as we were sure our services would be needed to get others up the grade from Ashton as the snow piled up. It snowed all night and gave us the splendor of bright sun on the crest of a new fallen foot of white fluff.

The burgers were superb, as was the memory I observed out the window while watching the flow of water I had floated on for miles in our old rubber rafts, down through Railroad Ranch to the old Osborne Springs Bridge where we pulled out.

My wife, Colleen, has her stories. She lived and worked in IP for years at Phillips Lodge, Pond's Lodge and a variety of other places when her first husband worked the highways for the Idaho Department of Transportation. This last Saturday we had been up putting a finishing touch on the family cabin before the long, deep snows of winter. Her grandparents first secured the land there in 1936 and built the sturdy dwelling over the years. She and I only realized our connection to Island Park after a chance meeting in Sandpoint, before we lost our respective spouses to cancer, and long before our own connection and eventual marriage. It's a connection we treasure, as we treasure our separate but enchanted recalls of that magical plateau just below Heaven.

# Ross Park and the Drive-In

When I read the headline "Ross Park Drive-In opens for the year," memories filled my afternoon. Early spring during my college days, young lady friends would call me from Graveley Hall on the campus of Idaho State University, asking if I could transport them to Ross Park Drive-In for (non-authentic) tacos. The tacos were great, and generous, which suited hungry girls on an outing from studies. My Oldsmobile would be crammed with sorority girls (not a bad thing) as we headed to this mecca of affordable fare.

Recently visiting Ross Park Drive-In, the owner asked my wife if I knew the year it was built. I did not. It's been there in one version or another since I can recall, in my mind, the early 1950s. To my surprise, I cannot find the original date of construction at any history source I searched.

This legendary hamburger stand will live forever as a favorite of railroad workers, college students, and employees of south-end businesses. Anyone going to the lower level of Ross Park passes within feet of the Drive-In. It's a no-brainer; if close by, the kids will scream from the back seat, "Corn dogs!" The menu items are as famous as the Drive-In itself, featuring Taco Spaghetti. A healthy portion comes in a large, foil-covered bowl; my nephew assures me it is wonderful!

Like many towns, Pocatello had grand burger joints, including standouts such as Fred and Kelly's, The Polar Bear,

Don Lemon's, Arctic Circle, Hawkins Red Steer, and the Tasty Treat across from the old cemetery.

Ben Ross, a Pocatello mayor, became Idaho's governor. In 1932, as governor, Ross ensured funds were appropriated for securing land along the railroad yards in the city's south end. The area was raw, untamed sagebrush land when Parks Director William Raymond was given the task of bringing the governor's dream to fruition.

The upper and lower parks are joined by a low lava plateau. Connecting both, narrow wooded trails weave past ancient lava outcroppings.

In infancy, the animal exhibit was called Zoo Idaho. Growth brought a music pavilion, where families were treated to orchestral music on shady summer evenings. The pavilion is still in use today.

The park is gently sloped from the upper level. On one of these levels, I tried, on a dare from friends, to jump the canal below the picnic patio. Having written before about the disastrous incident, I summarize again. I picked up speed as I shot down the grade but lacked jump trajectory to clear the ditch. Landing in the ditch's dry bottom, broken wheelchair, my father's displeasure was already ringing in my ears.

On the north end of the lower level was a carnival area called Pleasure Land. All sorts of activities were at hand, including a shooting gallery. I was quickly limited to one, 10-shot round, because of my acumen in that arena.

Years ago, a man in Coeur d'Alene spoke of Ross Park. I remarked that my father had built the baseball diamonds and started organized baseball there. He scoffed, condescendingly acknowledged my assertion. Years later, I sent him a news clipping from the Idaho State Journal that read, "Fifty years ago today this paper visited H.L. Hancock at Ross Park, clearing land and constructing pitchers' mounds using a tractor. With help from the men of the Moose Lodge, Hancock will build the bleachers and dugouts." Dad, gaining support from the Jim Lease Oil Company and Judge Gus Carr Anderson, raised funding for what was to become Little League, Pony League, and Chief League baseball, all played on his creations. He coached and escorted winning teams to Richland, Washington, Provo, Utah, and other towns across the West. Gene Hancock, my cousin, was an All-Star pitcher under Dad, later scouted by the Saint Louis Cardinals. As a young man, Dad played in the Yellowstone League, a semi-pro team that traveled, playing in Idaho's farm country. We were a baseball family. One of my father's players later made it to the major leagues.

Displays expanded with growth. On the upper level is a scale replica of Fort Hall. Not far from that site lies a turn-of-the-century town square.

In 1958, a retired steam locomotive was permanently placed at the park. Number 2005 long served the Oregon Short Line Railroad Company, later to be owned by Union Pacific. Dad installed the last side sheets in the boiler, and an uncle engineered it to its final park resting place. An aquatic park, horseshoe pits, and new skateboard jumps are a short walk away.

As youngsters, the park, when we could get there, was a haven from the heat. Its glorious trees provided cool air on blistering days. The Portneuf River, just beyond the railroad crossing, offered a swelter-breaking swimming hole. This brought us alongside hobo camp. Another story for another time.

Photo: Ross Park Drive-In.

# Freya, Jessie, Horses and Love

I call them my two Palomino girls (blondes), both equally as beautiful in childhood as they are today. Both are outstanding members of society that have earned their own places in the sun. Both are examples of hard work, dreams, and rock-headed perseverance until their goals were attained. Neither one came from a position of privilege or advantage, but both had the sheer determination it takes to beat the odds against a near-insurmountable uphill task, achieving their goals of being horsemen.

On a visit to our house on Trestle Creek, a seven-year-old named Freya came up to me with a garter snake in hand, held it out for me to take, and said, "Snakes are really good, people should not hurt them." I agreed, saying, "Now, for its benefit, put it back gently along the stream bed." She did so with loving care. Her father, besides being my lead carpenter for more than twenty years, was a great amateur herpetologist, having grown up in warm, dry environs. His knowledge was extensive and was passed on to his children. She grew up in a small house built by her family, off grid, in the deep snow country of upper Gold Creek in Bonner County, Idaho.

Horses were her passion from as early as I can recall. To acquire and keep her first horse, she went to work at the famous Woods Western Pleasure Ranch, a few miles down the road from her home. Her work there was the same as any hand on the ranch: mucking out stalls, moving manure, feeding, general clean-up, and care for the many equines that roamed the large pastures. No better education exists than in the field, training with horsemen that know their business.

Her talents were obvious from the beginning; she had what I call "hands." One of those special people, who can accomplish more with a touch of the hand than others can do with hours of training. Horses can feel a fly on their back, and Freya understood the feel and touch relationship, which gave her a hand up in training. It wasn't long until she was competing in horse shows and rodeo events. She and I fought some battles against unfairness on her way up the circuit.

As she grew, her beauty did as well, turning heads whenever she entered a room. Her talent brought her Queen status in numerous rodeos and horse events, culminating in Miss Pro-West Rodeo, Miss Rodeo Idaho, and then to the top of the heap, 1st runner-up to Miss Rodeo America in 2010. From there it was onwards and upwards. She made her own line of western wear, graduated with honors from college, and entered the world of agribusiness in a big way. Today, she owns her own piece of God's North Idaho ranch land where she raises kids and other critters, who will benefit no end from the touch of those hands.

About the time Freya was moving on at her university, I came home one day to see a thirteen-year-old girl, sopping wet, with an old white horse, Roanie, standing in snow, draped in a parka, slippers, and pajamas! She was visiting her dad and horse. Roanie was in tight quarters at her father's place in the woods. I opened my van window and speaking slowly said, "Girl, have you got rocks in your head?" It was cold and wet, as early spring days tend to be along the north shores of Lake Pend Oreille. She looked at me with big, soft eyes, dripping blonde hair, and a shyness that stood out, saying nothing. I had been feeding her horse apples each day, to keep her nutrition up and the cold at bay.

After I met Jessie that spring day, we both knew our paths would be linked from then on. Her life map was anything but certain and constant. Jessie once suggested I hire her boyfriend to work around my house Over my objections, she convinced me. As it turned out, Bennett is the finest of young men. He and Jessie were married in 2013, with me officiating. They now have a boy, destined to follow in his mother's horse world.

Jessie started out small, parlaying her horse sense into a career. She first, somehow convinced a banker to lend her money to buy a horse acreage, with an old barn and equally old house. Her training and riding school blossomed from there. She had that hidden quality both she and Freya share, creating a bond between horse and rider that blends them as one. Today, she runs a boarding facility/training stable booked with clients far into the future.

Young women who defied the odds. With pure guts and conviction, both created a world they desired and enabled others in doing so.

If you knew their stories in entirety, you would applaud them as I do. Having *grit* and *sand* are characteristics of this lifestyle, both of them have a whole lot of *try* thrown in. Against towering odds, these gifted horsewomen never gave up! A trait we desperately need more of today.

Photos: Freya and Jessie.

Note: The old white horse, Roanie, lived to almost 40 years old.

*Tales from the High Lonesome*

L. Scott Hancock

# Brain Sweeping

My wife and her son, who flew in from Spokane for the holiday, had gone to the store in town when the Amber Alert came over my phone, warning me of a white squall soon to hit the area. We were warned locally to shelter in place.

The squall came and went. Yes, it was bad for half an hour, but certainly not bad enough to warrant an Amber Alert warning. But then I got to thinking maybe they did it for all the newcomers that have moved in, who have never dealt with snow in that theatrical mecca south of Oregon. Sounds plausible. I couldn't understand the alert, when it seemed just as bad many times over the past two days. In fact, it resembled more like the S.E. Idaho I grew up in.

In my youth, we were sent home on numerous occasions when the school heating system wouldn't keep it warm at 30 below for five days! But the old grade schools that had steam radiator heat stayed comfortably warm. School districts, like so many other government entities, were thrilled to upgrade to new technology and modern electric hall furnaces. I went to Highland High School in Pocatello, its first year of operation. The glass fronts and open look were appealing, until it came time to heat the rooms. All-electric, floor-mounted, cabinet-like hall furnaces were all the rage at that juncture in time. Electric wall banks were the only place you could stay warm, if you were sitting on top of the unit. The storefront glass, single paned, was also a really stupid idea. They were warned by knowledgeable folks on the school board, but the powers that be forged ahead in their folly. Within a short time, the taxpayer once again was tapped for an upgrade to the heating and window system, "because these conditions could not have been foreseen." Hogwash! Am I bitching about unnecessary expenditures by government? You better believe it. The foolishness and limited vision of a few are colliding with common good sense folks with disastrous effects.

Case in point: the proposed near thirty-mile fencing to protect wildlife from entering the highway in Island Park. Oh boy! It would provide wildlife overpasses along the route, to take animals from one side of the highway to the other! WHAT A DEAL! I don't think so. Ken Watt, my friend and a brilliant, retired engineer, has been fighting this battle with far better solutions for years. Will the people of Island Park win? I don't know; these outside groups that are taking over our beloved land have cash to throw at stupid ideas by the wheelbarrow full. It irritates me no end that they believe their part-time summer living along the lake gives them insight into the everyday workings of people trying to live and make a living in the area especially when their half-baked plans are so full of flaws.

The squall has subsided, and now the skies are blue and cold. It is as Idaho should be. My Uncle Ward used to say, "If you don't like the weather in Idaho, wait five minutes, it'll change." Sound advice from a farmer who worked the land for seventy years.

We need to listen to the land, and the people who have its welfare at heart. They are not fools. It seems to me that much of the decision-making process today is strictly based on propaganda, rather than logic and solid information. I am not sure how much egalitarian attitudes are in play as we move forward.

When I was in college, we fought and screamed for free speech on campus. Now, even comedians will not go to campuses and present their shows, for fear of being shouted down with the insane political correctness that permeates our quasi-educational havens of today. How dangerous is that?!

I must say this as I clean my brain of festering thoughts. Our current guilty verdicts by TV talking heads have left the justice system weakened and marginalized in obtaining a balanced verdict. We are creating verdicts in the court of public opinion, and if the public doesn't see that as a serious danger, then God help us.

In finale, I want to leave you with my wishes for the New Year. I am not a cranky old fart (well maybe, according to my wife), I just want better, fairer ideals for all of us. The only way I see that happening is if we enlist some of those old magic ideals we learned as children. Consideration, equal justice under the law, and compassion for those in need, and for those who have suffered needlessly. Too often it is the innocents that pay. I'm trying to get this year in my rearview mirror and forget the idiots that speak to me from the tube and the podium. Hmm? Maybe I am an old crank, but I'm cranky about consummate greed and injustice; is that wrong? Happy New Year.

L. Scott Hancock

# Common Threads and Ken

I wrote an article about the famous photographer Ross Hall of Sandpoint, Idaho. The article was read by longtime friend Helen Newton, who forwarded it to legendary Sandpoint High School teacher and writer Marianne Love. Marianne has been retired a while now but not idle. Her many books are filled with wit, homespun humor, and honesty. My mother enjoyed them immensely and passed them on to her sisters, all farm ladies from southeastern Idaho. Well, it gets lots better from here. Marianne has a blog she writes each day for hundreds of followers. Not long after the article, my wife awakened me to show me that Marianne had made my story the topic of her daily blog. I was, as the kids would say, "blown away." She had written an article about Ross Hall years before, and was pleased another writer had his own shared tale. The plot thickens.

Ken Watt, writer for the *Island Park News* and retired engineer, emailed me saying he had worked for Marianne's father, haying and doing other farm chores, when he was a kid in Sandpoint. Old friendships renewed because of my Ross Hall story.

My relationship with Ken began when I still lived on the banks of Trestle Creek, in his childhood home of Bonner County. I had long been following Ken's articles about proposed drastic changes for the Island Park area. As a subscriber to the *Island Park News* and longtime lover of everything the area gave me as a child, and my father's heritage time spent there, my devotion to I.P. and its welfare are tantamount to obsession.

Ron Raiha, my old Pend Oreille Sports Shop friend, after reading Marianne's article, called to tell me how much his family loved Marianne as a teacher, a sentiment I heard countless times from others as the week wore on. Ron gave me another twist in this convoluted tale: "Scott, old Harold Tibbs, Marianne's father, came into the sports shop at least once a week. I'll never forget one of his greatest stories. It seems Jim Brown (legendary Bonner County businessman and Schweitzer Ski Resort developer) directed a road to be built up the mountain to where the ski resort would eventually be. That fall, Harold decided to go up the new access lane through the forest to do some hunting. He came upon a bear that climbed an old rotted-out cedar stump. Harold dispatched the bear, but it fell into the hollow stump body and couldn't be reached. Harold then proceeded home to get his vintage chainsaw and cut the dead bear out of the stump hollow, later to become steaks and summer sausage." No sooner had Ron hung up the phone, than my brain rattled and I said aloud, "Oh, my God, HAROLD, of course I remember him! We shared lies about hunting for years." And now back to Ken.

I was so happy my article had rekindled an old friendship and had put a light on Ken and his great work for the residents of Island Park over the years. Many homeowners and year-round dwellers are unaware of what Ken has done to preserve the area, guaranteeing their ability to earn a living and keep their ever encroached-upon lifestyle. His countless hours of meeting attendance and source material reading, with written comment, should make him volunteer citizen of the past ten years. He keeps informed on all the upcoming proposals that could permanently change Island Park forever, and not for the good! Ken has been labeled with cringeworthy names and called a curmudgeon, all because he believes the people who work and live on the Island Park Caldera have a right to an opinion, as much right as do the east coast questionable environmentalists that propose the changes, using millions of dollars of their group cash backing their findings. Balderdash!

Ken led the charge on stopping Island Park from becoming a Monument Area. Why, you say? Had anyone read the fine print National Monument status had so many drastic actions built in that the folks living in I.P. would literally be forced out of making a living there! Though a strong supporter of good environmental stewardship, Ken recognized the open-ended narrative and blew the whistle on some of the groupies, who were meeting in private with county officials to decide the future of the area. He requested information under the Freedom of Information Act and exposed their skullduggery. Heads rolled as those involved were dismissed by County Commissioners.

Ken single-handedly exposed the foolhardy nonsense of a chain-link fence along both sides of the highway leading to Yellowstone, with wildlife overpasses "to protect wild animals from vehicles." Another insane proposal, when much smarter, environmentally sound solutions are available.

Lastly, Ken is fighting the battle for the year-round homeowner forcing county officials to put in place protections against weekend rental units being occupied by party groups, who respect no private land or ordinance laws. Why should they? People come in from God knows where and do exactly as they please with the "party house" they have rented.

The list goes on. We all owe Ken a great debt of gratitude for standing fast against political interests with marginal ideas and insane demands.

Ken, each year I select my own "Person of the Year Award" recipient. You are my choice for 2021, but don't expect a prize. Maybe lunch. Keep up the selfless hard work, it is not in vain. Your forthright diligence is respected, admired, and we are thankful.

# Is a Camel a HORSE?

With delusionary ideas running rampant these days, I thought to myself, could some of them be true? Boys are allowed to compete in girls' sports because they identify as girls. Boys can use girls' bathrooms because they identify as girls; same goes for gym dressing areas. Truly, I don't know how this works, to me plumbing is plumbing! So, I was thinking, if this is all true, can a camel become a horse, if it identifies as such?

In grade school, Mrs. Hayden taught us how to figure out which camel was which. One hump or two. She told us to lay the capital printed letter D on its back (flat side), and that would signify a Dromedary camel, or a single cylinder job. If we put the capital letter B on its flat side (back), that would tell us it's a Bactrian camel, or a two-cylinder model. A single- or double-cylinder camel can be identified by going back in time and watching Warner Brothers cartoons, that showed an x-ray vison cutaway of the pistons going up and down in the humps. Clearly, these images detail a single or dual cylinder camel.

Now, the camel is a very interesting creature. It can go for a month without water, live in cold weather, as well as the burning sands. It stores fat in the humps, for protection against the extreme heat and cold of the desert climate. When it does drink, it can suck up 52 gallons of water in three minutes. Wow! Camels eat the sparsest of shrubs or tree leaves when available. These Desert Ships can run at remarkable speed, while carrying extraordinary luggage on their one or two humps, depending on the capital letter camel it is. Their feet are soft and splay out to give them wide traction, keeping them from sinking into the sand.

The camel's counterpart, the great Arab horse, is speedy, intelligent, as are camels, and can carry great loads for its size and build. They are durable in the hot sand country. This breed is gorgeous with distinctive heads, solid dense bone structure, and great endurance over the long haul with remarkable stamina.

But is a horse a camel because it identifies as one? A science degree is not needed to tell us this is physiological insanity. Arab horses are capable of a couple of days, and a hundred miles, without water. It can't carry the weight nor live in the extremes of the camel. On the other side of the coin, the camel might want to look like the beautiful Arab to attract the opposite sex, but does that make it so? You get my point. What are we thinking, as a species supposedly capable of rational thought, carrying on with this silliness?

Along this same irrational line of thought, another question came up. If we so dangerously rewrite history, can we change the outcome that has already happened? Perhaps we should go back and ask the Vikings to not be so darn hard on people, require paper swords, rubber spears, and arrows. In this manner, our children wouldn't have to hear about all the bad things in history. We can just change it and make up our own version.

Let's examine this a bit more. Could we change the great conqueror Genghis Khan if we offered him a seat for group therapy or, better yet, a mat in a hot yoga class? If so, class would go something like this:

"Mr. Khan, welcome to our group." Khan replies, "Urgh!" "Mr. Khan, perhaps you would feel better on the folding chair if you put down your spear and undid your sword belt. I know the class would feel more comfortable, right class?" The class replies in unison, "Oh, yes, instructor, we would feel better and safer." "Okay, what do you say to that, Mr. Khan?" Genghis looks at his armament and replies, while holding the hilt of his sword, "Urgh." "Thank you, Mr. Khan. As you can see this will make our class and history of this day much easier for future generations to assimilate, without the thought of violence or that it might occur or ever has occurred. Simply put, we'll act as though all the bad stuff never happened, therefore changing fact into fiction." "Oh, and Mr. Khan, before you march out hurriedly onto your next conquest, could you pause for a moment to participate in a group hug?"

At this juncture, Mr. Khan draws his sword, and mayhem ensues. The next day, it was reported in the news headlines: "Violent sword causes severe damage to chairs and yoga mats in group therapy class. The class was trying to re-create Mr. Khan's unenlightened regrettable past, creating a new history, more warm, fuzzy and palatable, when the sword went berserk."

I started thinking, could this type of re-imagining work for me, having spent most of my life using crutches and wheelchairs? What if I imagined myself striding along the path, wind trailing through my hair; would it happen? I'll get back to you on that.

# Mary M.

"She showed up at the beach on her motorcycle, got off, and grabbed a six-pack of beer from the back. We were holding some sort of women's organization event. That was my first experience with Mary McFarland," my old friend Helen Newton recalled while describing a vintage Mary encounter.

From Gotthard Pass in Switzerland, to the steps of Jefferson's Monticello, to Alaska, or wherever she is currently, riding the phantom sky, I can hear her cussing me for the following story, saying "that never happened," but it did.

While waiting for my own motorcycle to be serviced at Sandpoint's best cycle shop, old friend Roger rode in on his BMW, followed shortly after by Mary. Wearing her buckle motorcycle boots, blue jeans, and an old T-shirt, she looked like a biker from a 1950s Marlon Brando movie, her skin leathery with years of farm and ranch work ingrained, her hair very short, voice low and clear. Her T-shirt sleeve held a pack of hand-rolled cigarettes. She lit up using her custom Zippo lighter and asked, "What's going on?" That image is chiseled in time. In a leather holster on the bike frame was her 357 Magnum pistol. In her early sixties at that time, she was still a pretty woman, tough as she looked and absolutely fearless. Mary was beyond legend, she was an iconoclastic enigma.

I recalled recently our first meeting in Boise, attending a conference addressed by then-Governor Andrus. When the governor finished, he asked for comments. Mary, putting down her whiskey glass, stood, saying, "I don't know about the rest of you (expletive deleted), but here is what I think." Jaws dropped. I laughed. I knew we had to meet. After introducing myself, she treated me cordially but was not interested in chitchat. Having ridden to Boise on her motorcycle, she wanted to get home to her ranch near Clark Fork, Idaho. She once told me the blacksmith on her father's wheat ranch had taught her to smoke, cuss, and drink, all of which she carried on with marvelous alacrity to the end, with moderation.

Leaving her mother's home in Spokane as a girl, she walked to a grain elevator, hitching a ride on a wheat truck south to the Washtucna, Washington prairie, and her father's wheat farm. At each elevator she caught another southbound truck to the Rattlesnake Hills where the farm was located. Upon arrival, Mary told her father if he sent her back, she would run away. Her father knew Mary and recognized the truth, a trait she carried the rest of her life. She spoke intelligently, honestly, and absolutely straight.

Graduating from Washington State University with honors in music, Mary and beau Glenn married. He fought in the South Pacific aboard the famous battlecruiser Lexington. She worked as a Rosie the Riveter in a plant back home. At war's end, both became pilots, following Glenn's career with the Aviation Administration to airport assignments across the West. Mary initiated her own flying service, flying anything and everything allowed. Flying grid patterns for mapping directed by the State of Wyoming, her notoriety grew. She flew solo around the West, and cross-country in Powder Puff Derbies. Typical of Mary, when she and Glenn disagreed once on a flight plan, she opened the plane window and threw the maps out, saying, "Okay, find it yourself." On several occasions, their daughter, Sarah, thought death was imminent during some of Mary's exploits.

The McFarlands purchased ranch land in North Idaho upon Glenn's retirement, and raised cattle. Then came motorcycles. The first, an old dirt bike she bought at a bar over beers. She ran that one into the Clark Fork River! The passion grew to more than thirty bikes in her lifetime, with trips all over Europe, Alaska, and across the Lower 48 countless times. There were accidents and outlandish events, but her love grew for two-wheeled rockets. Her handwritten stories appeared in motorcycle magazines across the country. Adventures and politics led her to befriend many interesting and famous individuals, and yes, she knew Eleanor Roosevelt!

WSU finally, honored Mary, for her sports achievements from so many years before, with a Platinum Alumnus Award Dinner, installing her in the University's Hall of Fame.

Holding her hand not long before she died in her 95th year, I said, "Mary, it's Scott." She squeezed with that familiar strong, ranch hand clench. I drifted back through all the years I had known and loved this woman, and the countless projects on their ranch the family gave me. The memories of her unbelievable life and adventures should fill many books, and I hope someday they will. For now, when I look at the old horse-drawn hay mower from their ranch that adorns the drive up to our house or hold one of her favorite rifles in my hands, I dream while I wipe the smiles from my eyes.

Photos: Mary, on her late in life, XLS Harley Trike.

# Spring Forward and Elisa

My father-in-law once asked Orrin Hatch, retired US Senator from Utah, "Why don't you guys just get rid of Daylight Saving Time?" Senator Hatch told him, "It will never happen because congressmen want that extra daylight on the golf greens." That seems like the most honest answer I have ever heard to explain this mindless, costly nonsense!

First proposed by Ben Franklin as a joke; to outline the laziness of his fellow aristocratic constitutional framers, it sadly became law and a damned nuisance. I do understand that lots of folks like it, I do not, and we'll leave it at that. To me, it smacks too much of other things that are not natural. Something else manipulated that was better off left as it was. Yes, in almost all cases, I am a naturalist, meaning "If it ain't broke, don't fix it!" But politicians need to have something to occupy their time besides blaming the other side of the aisle. My take anymore is much like the great American humorist Will Rogers' outlook on politics: "It's a good thing we don't get all the Government we pay for."

The voice of the people seems less and less important each year. The folks in Boise and Washington DC tell us daily how much they care, and how hard they are working- BALLDERDASH! And now the Crazy Season, as former Idaho Governor Cecil Andrus called it, has begun. I'm seeing stupid ads from newcomers seeking office, who have hired some political consulting firm to create lies that seem plausible to the average voter. And there is the problem. The average voter is often kept below average in awareness by these vermin, on purpose. People don't have time to challenge these ads and their deceitful perpetrators. Voters tend to follow party lines, with a minimum of knowledge about the truth of the issue their voting on. It frustrates me no end! Will Rogers put it this way: "It ain't what we don't know that gives us trouble, it's what we know that ain't so."

Ken Watt wrote two stories recently in the *Island Park News* that should have every resident, visitor, and frequent driver alarmed about the future of highway travel from Ashton, Idaho, to West Yellowstone, Montana. The roadway running through this gorgeous natural area is facing future insane changes using outdated data, and predictions based on "reasonable guesses." The Big Boys in Boise, sitting behind their desks at the Idaho Transportation Department, are listening to engineering firms with grandeur in mind at taxpayers' expense, using inadequate data instead of listening to the people and the elected officials of Fremont County and the surrounding areas.

Changes coming to the Island Park area are truly alarming, both from a state level and from local officials listening to their in-house professional planners instead of their constituents. With Yellowstone Park becoming more and more visitor-besotted, and less visitor-friendly, these changes in traffic patterns will have overwhelming impacts for all who travel the highway to that wonderful, otherworldly destination called Yellowstone. Read and digest what politicians are saying, never trust a bureaucrat without firsthand knowledge, and never vote on a subject just because some political party hack tells you to.

And now, an update on Elisa. Readers of my books or my columns know my love for Elisa (E.C. Stilson), author, prolific writer, and columnist for the *Island Park News*. She was the editor/publisher at the *Blackfoot Morning News* who encouraged me to write more columns, which brought me to this point. So many of my readers questioned me as to her health and progress, I knew it was time to share my knowledge.

For new readers, Elisa was diagnosed with cancer just after she published my first book. It took us all by surprise, but knowing Elisa as one of a kind, I knew she would carry on in the most gracious of manner. And she has! I cannot count the trips to the Huntsman Cancer Center in Salt Lake, nor can she, I'm sure. But she goes on, with the most remarkable attitude and strength, and an overwhelming love and sharing for all around her.

So many readers have seen her playing her violin for patients at Huntsman's while balancing herself with a walker. I re-watch these performances on YouTube to gain personal perspective. They give me an even deeper love for this girl, her family, and the precious gifts she gives freely. My first communication each morning is to her in the form of a text. Before the day is out, she will fill me in on her and her family's plans, and fun they had together. Her model of life lived, and giving, under difficult circumstances, has led me to a higher place in my own observance of a place to be in this stratosphere. In short, she makes me transcend my earthly boundaries.

I asked you all for your prayers, and you gave them freely to Elisa. For this, I am humbled and grateful. She goes on with style and grace that all of us can see and adopt. Her daily routine is filled with challenges that take great effort to overcome, but overcome she does, and moves on in love and faith, guiding others with cancer on their personal journeys. And now, sweet girl, you have a publisher for your story of resilience and giving during this trial. Congratulations!

Know this angel on earth: many have come to know and love you through your writings and other social media. Each day, people send their prayers skyward on your behalf. For Mike, your grand husband, and those delightful, crazy, wonderful kids, remember you too are loved. May God bless and keep you always.

# Parking Decorum

Dick Marler, who wrote a column for the *Island Park News*, was a master of sly wit and off-handed humor. His columns were filled with simple observations of life around him, situated in his mind, and given to us with a smile. He reminded me greatly of the casual yet compound humor of Will Rogers. In my column in the *Island Park News* recently, recalling recent parking lot interactions, I received lots of comments from readers asking for more of my vision involving indiscretions carried on by unthinking, or uncaring, folks who "just don't give a damn." I'm no Dick Marler, but maybe I can create a smile with the following.

Yesterday, I made my third trip to Idaho Falls in as many days. I would rather be bludgeoned with a dull Stone Age ax than drive 17$^{th}$ Street one more time. I'm sure any visitor to I.F. shares my lack of enthusiasm for this avenue. One simply puts their lives in the hands of others, hoping the others are good Christian drivers with an understanding people need to use this god-awful street to arrive at a prescribed destination.

Arriving at a megastore to pick up a new computer for my wife's Christmas present, I had no option but to park in a handicapped parking space. I try not to do this, as there are so many folks more in need of these spots than I. Often, we see people with no outward signs of disability, but disabled they are, with lung conditions, weak hearts, or failing bone structures. It is obvious that they have an issue, and I am more than happy to relegate a spot to them.

And now to my personal greatest 'bitch' in this displayed lack of decorum. While sitting in my spot, a jacked-up pick-up truck pulled in directly in front of me in another handicapped parking space. I kid you not, out jumped two twenty-somethings who ran into the store! Neither one had a hint of any problems whatsoever. Upon returning, they climbed back into the truck using the side steps and sped off. There is no way a physically-challenged individual could have negotiated entry into this behemoth rock climber. How they came by a handicapped placard to hang in their window is beyond me. My guess, they borrowed it from someone, although some MDs today will sign a disability permit certificate if the applicant shows an allergy to milk chocolate.

This egregious behavior causes me no end of stomach acid reflux, as my anger builds to the point of vaporization status! I knew of a man in a wheelchair who broke out headlights and taillights of violators parked in disabled access parking spots. He was arrested many times and released, paying restitution for his breakages. I and others sent him money for bail. The violators, too, paid dearly with the presiding judge who oversaw the cases. Soon, the small-town wheelchair superstar celebrated no more parking cheaters. Having fought my entire life for those with special needs, it does my old liver good to see the headway made in the last 50 years. By and large, people are more than willing to respect the adaptations made to accommodate folks who march with a different flute and flag.

More than a few readers addressed this next issue: Idiots who gas up their motor vehicle and leave it parked at the pumps, while they go into a store to shop!

My nephew told me of one he encountered in Rocker, Montana. Anyone who has been to Rocker knows it's a spot in the road for lodging, food, and all-night service with these conveniences and fuel. Dozens of semi-truck loads come in and out each hour, as do drivers of the open road. It seems a motorhome with a small car in tow pulled in next to one set of pumps, taking up an entire side of the available fuel station. Filled with fuel, the driver left the motorhome parked next to the pumps while he went into the truck stop. Waiting patiently, my nephew thought he would return presumably after paying his bill or picking up a quick soft drink. He did not. My nephew went in after pulling his truck to a different set of pumps, filling up, and then parking in the lot nearby. Once inside the truck stop the motorhome driver was seen leaving the restaurant, with food in hand he had ordered and waited for. The entire process took almost an hour. OMG! These incidents are rash creators for my friend Ken, who also writes for the *Island Park News*.

    I have personally witnessed here in Blackfoot an incident much like the one in Rocker. A motorhome, with an attached trailer full of four wheelers, parked at the pumps in a small station for over thirty minutes while they ate lunch inside. Guess where they were from? We are told not to judge by home state license plate or parking behavior. But I do both, gleefully smiling while trying to retain my calm, demure nature, remembering my friend with his penchant for breaking out lights. Tongue in cheek, I say, "Shame on him!"

*L. Scott Hancock*

# Shadow People

When, on rare occasions while growing up, my parents and I went to downtown cafés for burgers, or the folks to have coffee and cocoa for me, there were always the same people who seemed to be in their regular seats hunched over coffee. Sometimes, reading the paper, often filling in crossword puzzles. I didn't know then that these people had 'family' in those restaurants. The staff and friends who came by daily were their family. It was years later I learned where some of these shadow people lived, and how they made it through their days.

One of the first who came into focus was Watermelon Charlie, who lived in the back of Eve's Café on Center Street in Pocatello, Idaho. Charlie's life is painted in part in my first book of *Tales*. Charlie was one of those folks I think we describe now as "fallen through the cracks." A euphemistic way of saying they don't fit in.

Old Bill in Coeur d' Alene was much the same. Each day as I wheeled down 4$^{th}$ Street to my job, in the old Wigett Building, he would disappear behind a door that led to the bowels of that building, below the sidewalk level. Bill lived in the basement boiler room of that old three-story beauty, that was the first in town to have an elevator. One day, Bill allowed me to look down the stairway to the basement. I was brain claustrophobic as I stared. The stairway was just wide enough to descend, if you turned your shoulders sideways a bit. Later, a friend and owner of the building told me Bill had lived there since they were in high school together, because he had no place else. His adoptive parents had died and left Bill alone.

Bill took over maintenance chores for the building and became Coeur d' Alene's own Phantom, living alone with his radio and small TV, only coming out on the sidewalk to quickly enter a side door that took him into the main part of the building. The two other times Bill came out were for food at the old Merrill's Café, and for church on Sunday. We became friends, but like so many others in life's lane, you lose track of their lives when moves take you elsewhere.

Yesterday, I was in Pocatello, moseying along the streets towards what is now called Antique Alley. Fashionable antique stores now occupy the old Woolworth's and other Main Street stores of the day. Stores that became delights in my childhood. It surprises me every time I'm on Main Street as to how little the current occupant/renters know about the area they now inhabit. Looking out across the street to a two-story rock building façade, I read the word "Carlyle."

As I read the raised stone letters, I remembered Sandy. Sandy lived upstairs in the Carlyle when I was a kid. Every day he did chores to pay for his coffee and food at the Old Timers Café on Main. A favorite of railroad workers, it was crowded any time of day. Countless times I watched rail workers pick up Sandy's ticket, paying for it along with their own. In those days it seemed every town had shadow people that other folks respected and cared for.

One Christmas back in Pocatello, spending the holidays with my family, I went downtown shopping. It was cold as hell as Pocatello is that time of year, with the ever-present breeze making the cold colder. I went into the Old Timers for coffee and pie. Not long into my coffee sipping, with a second bite of pie in hand, I looked up as the cold wind blew in through the doorway to see a very gray and stooped Sandy. He was greeted by a whole new set of rail employees and downtown regulars. My heart gladdened.

The little town of Rathdrum, northeast of Coeur d'Alene, had its own special character in Sarge. Sarge was really Bobby, who performed a variety of tasks for locals, strong as a bull with a gentle soul. Each night Bobby went around to the local bars, where he was fed and given Shirley Temples, as he filled the revelers with the doings of the town. When Sarge entered these establishments, wearing his trademark Cavalry hat with sergeant stripes, his greeting was much like Norm's on the TV show "Cheers." Everyone yelled, "Bobby!" and watched the grin fill his face as he waved a greeting. Bobby lived on the edge of polite society, as they like to think of themselves, and was loved beyond any measure of what the local elite could ever hope to obtain.

And now, in Blackfoot, I see the same people sitting at the morning coffee counter in Martha's Café, or across the street getting tacos at El Vaquero, or down the street a bit further at Smokin' Gun BBQ. They are the same people, just different towns with different names. Every community has shadow people. Finding a public family that accepts them, expecting nothing more than a nod, small talk, and a smile over a plate while morning coffee aroma steams the air, they slide into place where they belong.

# Winter Story

"Hello, are you awake?" Yawning, I whispered back, "I am now!" As the conversation progressed, I looked over at the bedside clock, the red digits on the screen reading 5:05 a.m. "Can you meet me at the Holiday Shores at 7:00?"

My head was cleaning out cobwebs of a deep sleep when I asked, "Kevin, what the hell is going on?" "Somebody broke through the ice last night in a vehicle, joyriding around Ellisport Bay, and is at the bottom of the lake now!" The lake was Pend Oreille, in Bonner County, Idaho. The caller was Kevin Keating, local reporter for the *Spokesman-Review* newspaper out of Spokane, the same Kevin who wrote the back page introduction for my first book. Kevin was stationed in Sandpoint, Idaho, as the *Spokesman*'s bureau chief in the office there. As the fog cleared, my attention span lengthened, and I asked, "Any idea who it was?" "Yes, but I gotta run, my phone is ringing off the hook. I'll fill you in when we get to the Holiday Shores Café."

Getting up for me is a slow process at best—strapping on leg braces, clothes, getting into the chair, and wheeling out the door is not Secretariat running a race. It's more like the tortoise and the hare vying for first place, me being the tortoise. But that morning I scrambled to get to my van and meet Kevin, introducing him to the locals so he could get the scoop on what had happened the previous evening. Sheriff's deputies and divers were all around the parking lot when I arrived, and my god, it was cold! I looked at the thermometer mounted just outside the café door; it read 5 degrees. Once inside, I got the story long before Kevin arrived. Two locals, after a night of revelry, decided to go car sliding on a frozen-over Ellisport Bay, not far from a local bar. The ice was at least five inches thick, and locals had indulged in this insanity many times in the past. Why these two broke through was to remain a mystery until later.

As I entered the café, Captain Fred and his son Bobby Kennedy met me, and I joined them at their table. The café was jam-packed with locals standing around holding coffee, sharing stories about the ice, its thickness, and asking, "How the hell did they break through?"

Captain Fred spoke in his quiet, measured manner, "They think it was Marty Kiebert and Doobie Anderson." Kevin arrived, talking to the deputies and divers in the parking lot. It appeared the guys in the bay had launched their car from Holiday Shores boat ramp, proceeding out to the middle, spinning around and around until the ice gave way.

As the morning wore on, more people crowded in, awaiting any confirmation as to the location of the car and its passengers. Divers were in and out quickly; the conditions were not favorable for locating or seeing below the surface. The ice was so thick that the lake became black just a few feet below the frozen layer. Drinking buddies of the two Ice Capade spinners confirmed the identities of those in the incident. Apparently, the idea of lake ice spinning in a car had been a bar topic the night before, but no one thought these two would really go through with it. Numerous people had spoken strongly against the plan, but went on home, giving it no more credence.

In the middle of the night, many of them were awakened by the Sheriff's office. Deputies were seeking information in ascertaining the identities of the vehicle occupants. As the day wore on, TV crews from Spokane showed up and interviewed people who were willing to share their story slant on camera. I remember declining an offer to speak; it was not in my conscience to spin these sad, unnecessary deaths. Marty's niece worked on my construction crew, and I knew most of the family.

As the morning wore on, the divers found a car and were able to free the two occupants from their seats, bringing them to the surface. I won't describe what one of the divers told me about how they found the victims. It haunts me to this day.

Late in the day, it was learned that two days before, a tugboat with a barge in front broke the ice as it left the harbor for a local mission. This tug-broken ice left an open channel to freeze back over. The channel is where the car fell through and sank. Had a couple more days passed, this open channel would have frozen thick enough to once again support a car. Left undisturbed, the ice would probably have frozen hard enough to hold the revelers, allowing them later to regale in their hazardous adventure.

Days later, the car was pulled from the bottom using the tug and barge operation. A crane on the barge lifted the sedan to the surface. I watched as thousands of gallons of water drained from the automobile. It was then carefully placed on the barge by a local, skilled crane operator. If there is a moral to this story, maybe it's for young readers. The ice may not always be as thick as you might imagine. Proceed with caution and never trust your judgment about anything after a few rounds at the local watering hole!

*L. Scott Hancock*

# More Boots, Less Beans

A while back, I wrote an article for The *Island Park News* about the legendary (in cowboy minds) western cartoonist, Boots Reynolds. I put the article and photos of some of his cartoons in a subsequent book. There's the rub. I was told by the publisher they could not print the cartoon photos without permission from the artist. Well, that presented a problem. Boots' wife, the long-suffering Becky, had shed North Idaho not long after Boots joined Will Rogers, Mark Twain, and others around that big campfire of humorists in the sky. We lost track of each other for a bit. But I finally, through old friends, found her to seek an okay for publishing the prints.

Becky was back living in Sandpoint, after some blue butt cold winters in Big Sky country. I used the word long-suffering to describe Becky. Let me shed some light on that phrase. Becky was married to Boots (Roy) Reynolds forever. That, in and of itself, qualifies her for sainthood! Boots was full bore on life, and his humor filled every minute. He was the funniest man I personally have ever met, and when, God forbid, we were together, it was shameless. Becky reminded me of one grand scene Boots and I created in a Sandpoint restaurant over Sunday breakfast. I was so happy for her to recreate the tale, because I had completely forgotten the event.

I smile again as I write this; it was vintage Boots. It goes something like this... My wife and I were seated, awaiting our meal, when Boots and Becky came in and sat across the room. Before I proceed, I need to tell you my wife, now departed, was a proper Swiss Lady, with a strong sense of decorum, an attribute neither Boots nor I had a smidge of in our bloodlines. We were both cow pasture creations who had been around the greats of Western lore. Also, I need to explain that the eatery was an old house that had two rooms from which one could choose to dine in.

Boots started the trouble right off by hollering, "Hey Scooter, how ya been?" He never could remember anyone's name. I was Scooter, Shooter (from my pool shooting days), or Speedy depending on his mood. "I've been faring well, and you?" "Oh, pretty much the same. This time of year reminds me of ranching and things that need taking care of when the snow finally melts." The conversation went downhill from this point. I blamed Boots later in the day to my wife, but she was having no part of it. She asked, "What did you think I was doing when I kicked you under the table?" "Well, I thought you were having a spasm or something. How was I to know you were displeased?" A little clarity is needed here to set the scene correctly—only one other table of diners was in our large room that morning, properly attired churchgoers, stopping by for brunch before heading home to the lawn mower and cooking Sunday family dinner.

"Yup, there's lots to be done around the place when the creek's busting its banks with runoff." Boots proceeded into a discussion of removing appendages off male animals come spring, using the dreaded "C" word. "Hell, Boots, I remember how some of the old sheep men did the job, and the Rocky Mountain Oyster Stew that came from the leavings." My wife looked at me and whispered, "Scott, people are trying to enjoy their meal!" I looked at her with a questioning eye, saying, "Yeah, I know."

But I didn't know! Apparently, our across the room discussion about operative procedures around ranch country was somehow offensive. The church folks in the middle of the room picked up their plates, moving to the other dining area out of sight and sound. My wife said, "Now, look what you've done!" I explained to her I was sure they just wanted more of the sunshine the opposite room offered. I still blame Boots for his leading me down the wrong road of conversation. When Becky reminded me of that day, I laughed till tears were running down my cheeks.

Boots was a hoot, no matter when you met him. His famous cartoon artistry lives on in the houses of hundreds of people. His funny-as-hell greeting card illustrations for Leanin' Tree and his gut-busting cartoons that graced the pages of *Western Horseman* and other magazines show pure genius. The American Cowboy Hall of Fame gave him a one-man retrospective show. (If you want to know more about Boots and his work, it's easy to find on the Internet.)

Becky sent the letter of permission to use his work in my writings, along with a very generous grouping of some of his most famous cartoon works, all of which will be mounted for display in my home. When I called to thank Becky, she asked if I had heard that Baxter Black had died. Baxter was the funniest cowboy lecturer and writer since Will Rogers, and a very close friend of Boots and Becky. As Becky said, "Baxter and Boots were cut from the same cloth." I met Baxter at a draft horse show in Bozeman. His wit was intoxicating and rattlesnake quick. With both of them in Cowboy Heaven folks will walk the straight and narrow here on Earth, just to ensure they end up on the right side of the clouds to laugh at those two again.

Photos, Boot's illustrations: "Happy Birthday from the Rest of the Hired Help"

# Up in Smoke

As I write this, my old home on Trestle Creek, in Bonner County, Idaho, is under mandatory evacuation as a fire surges up the ridge, threatening to join a fire on the other side of the mountain. If this fire joins the Flume Creek blaze, it's "Katy bar the door." North Idaho, as with much of the West, is as dry, if not worse, as the conditions that gave us the 1910 fire or the Big Blow Up. I spoke with an old neighbor on Creekside Lane: "It's bad, we all may lose everything, but by god I'll go down with the ship." And I expect he will; his family are pioneers in the area.

Fire is not merciful, it is not vengeful, it is consuming. As a boy, I watched fire go from one side of Marsh Creek, in southern Idaho, to the black rock lava that stopped it in thirty minutes. The distance? Almost a mile. I have been around and witnessed this natural phenomenon in many areas since childhood, including Island Park, Yellowstone, the Arco Desert, Northern Idaho, and dozens of other locales. Fire is somehow fascinating until you're in its path of destruction, then it becomes a death-dealing dragon moving quickly to engulf everything you hold dear. Evacuation has been in my life twice, both times in Kootenai County in North Idaho.

The 1910 fire started in northwestern Montana in April of that year. At the same time frame, Wyoming, Idaho, and Washington were dealing with local uncontrolled blazes. The Forest Service was barely five years old and woefully unequipped, in mindset and materials, to fight large conflagrations. Men and equipment were scarce, and by

August, the painful drought worsened. Conditions were prime for an all-out catastrophe. That came with a series of unrelenting wind storms that drove the fire in North Idaho to disaster status in just hours. By August 10$^{th}$ there were six national forests with uncontrollable fires. By August 20-21$^{st}$ the blazes were burning towns in North Idaho, and trains were being used to evacuate people. Half of the city of Wallace burned. Near Wallace, a courageous Forest Service Fire Boss, named Ed Pulaski, took his crew of 45 men into a mine shaft before they were overrun by the flames. He personally held blankets over the shaft entrance to stop the smoke. After directing the men to lie face down, he kept the entrance blocked until he was overcome. Pulaski, and 40 of his crew, survived and he became an immediate national hero, later credited with creating the axe-grub hoe combination known to this day as the Pulaski.

One of my first meetings as a staff member of the state agency that set up Senior Centers was in Wallace, I was invited to a dinner where the speaker was 94-year-old Dolly Parker. Dolly related how her father, in 1910, led his family to a nearby boarded-up mine shaft, where he broke the lock on the plank door. Safe inside, with the door blocking the flames and smoke, they huddled together until the next day. When they went out, the door was deeply burned, and half the town was gone! Not prepared for this gigantic inferno, the Forest Service pleaded for help. Finally, the President sent in 4000 troops to help stop the blazes, which burned from south of Wallace all the way north to Lake Pend Oreille and the Clark Fork River. In total, before the 1910 blazes were finished, the West lost 5 million acres. Smoke drifted to Chicago and eastward. Winter came, and those fires still burning were extinguished as the snow piled up in the forests.

My father worked fires in his youth, north and west of Ashton, Idaho. He told the story of 15 days straight working on a fire, sleeping on the ground, using shovels and grub hoes to create fire lines of open area to keep the blazes from jumping tree to tree. His only bath was when he jumped into a creek in his clothes to get everything washed at once. With fires comes smoke. My friend Blaze, in Sandpoint, told me today that the air was so thick it was difficult to breathe, and the cars in town had ash on them.

More than twenty years ago, the Forest Service let out contract bids to select cut timber in the Trestle Creek drainage. It has been stopped by an eco-group out of Spokane countless times, costing millions of dollars to the taxpayers fighting these lawsuits. Logging is essential at this point to saving the overall forest ecosystem. The Strong Creek canyon and Trestle Creek drainage in North Idaho are two prime examples of windfall and dead-standing tree buildup, waiting for the next lightning strike or careless match.

Is it smarter to practice good forest management or fire aftermath cleanup including some towns? What happened in California a few years ago, when an entire town burned up, could happen tomorrow in Sandpoint, Island Park, Pocatello, or Jackson Hole. It's coming whether we choose to believe it or not. Sadly, another town may burn before we wake up.

What's needed is to allow some small, controlled fires to burn, taking out windfall debris and undergrowth. In addition, keep the lands clear of massive stands of dead timber, using select cut logging and cleanup. When fires begin in forests with substantial windfall and debris, they create their own weather systems as massive flames grow, unleashing another series of problems. Unless sensible minds come together on good forest management, I fear the West will burn while selfish people play eco-politics. For now, pray for a long, hard rainstorm with no lightning.

L. Scott Hancock

# Parking Lot Wonders

The Big Box stores have become my favorite places to watch people. Well, not really the stores, but their parking lots. The biggest is one of America's conglomerate giants that sells everything under one roof. My idea of its usefulness is providing crochet aficionados with thousands of yards of colored string needed to make an afghan. I watch as people leave this store with shopping carts filled with bushels of bound, multi-colored string, destined for a new life as a couch cover or butt warmer, long-length sweater. At this point, a warning is in order: NEVER GO TO THESE STORES AROUND THE FIRST OF THE MONTH! It's payday.

I have never gone into this particular big box because of a personal dislike for all it represents, and the fact they hasten the demise of small mom and pop stores, unable to compete in product pricing. I do understand the purpose it serves and try not to pass judgment as I sit in the parking lot, smiling and laughing at the people with their kids, dogs, cars, shopping carts, and the management of these items in no particular order.

The parking lots of these mega mall stores provide an education, with humor thrown in, for the observer. Case in point, we had just pulled into our collective lot, when I came to full rest while a shopper walked by in front of us, destined to a nearby trunk waiting to carry home their bounty. On the sidewalk near the storefront was a darkly-tanned woman in what my wife describes as a sports bra, with a two-lace back and skintight workout pants, way too small for the torso. None of this covered any more of her large frame than was absolutely necessary to avoid arrest for indecent exposure. Trust me, I am not a prude, but this sight made me wonder if she had a mirror at home, or was this her statement against convention? In either case, she started scuffling with her paramour (I assume), and more of the abundant flesh was loosened as the tug-a-war continued. And so, she won my Parking Lot Vision of the Week award. It was stunning!

Camo clothing, I realize, is the new chic and begs to be worn everywhere, but is it really the thing to wear on a bitter cold day in Blackfoot? Let me create the optic.

I watched as a young man departed his car in full camo nightwear. Camo pajama top and bottom, camo sweatshirt, camo socks with camo slippers, camo cap, all in summer weight thickness. The man disappeared into the fabric of the parking lot quickly, not to be seen again until he returned with a shopping cart of beer. The beer was encased in a camo box container. I have no doubt waiting at home was a camo couch, TV, and bed with camo sheets, that made you disappear as you crawled between them to snuggle and sleep on your camo My Pillow.

Food choices are another of my favorite things to guess when a person parks nearby to go into the store. I have this down pat. If it's a Friday and a young guy in a jacked-up pickup shows up, his return cart will be filled with beer, chips, and frozen pizzas, all in preparation for the weekend TV football games. Except if he's in camo, then it's beer, jerky, chips, a can of chew, and some peanut M&Ms to wash it all down on the drive home.

Parking lots also afford a look at beautiful humanity. On numerous occasions I had seen a battered old pickup around town, with a makeshift camper shell on the back. I had never, until the other day, seen the owner of this pickup. A lot of space put me just two cars away from this vehicle. As I watched a small argument between a wife and husband about who was driving home, the owner of the pickup rolled into view. She appeared very frail and small, driving the electric scooter provided by the store. Every available space on the scooter was filled with household items and foodstuffs. I was in no position to disembark from my van, to help her load her groceries up over the tailgate of her truck and down into the bed. Just as I was going to holler over and tell her I would arrange help to load her goods, a young woman with child in tow approached her and offered assistance. The older woman accepted gladly. When the young lady finished loading the truck, I tooted my horn and gave her the thumbs-up sign. She smiled sheepishly and waved back to me. The older lady struggled up into the driver's seat and, ever so slowly, exited the lot. Every door panel and body corner had a dent, from lots of things that I suppose just jumped out to make her life harder. It was obviously hard enough. I drove away thinking of the older lady and the young mother and smiled. Life has its beautiful moments and moments of humor seen through a dirty windshield.

# Shorty's Scouts

Trading in his '64 Plymouth Fury, with the tire-burning motor, was a hard thing for brother Shorty to do, but he had his heart set on an International Harvester Scout four-wheel drive. Off to Blackfoot we went, me in the driver's seat so to speak, because he wanted me to get him a good deal on his trade-in and new rig.

Blackfoot was the nearest Corn Binder dealer. The showroom, as it was, stood directly across the street from the state fairgrounds corner. It is now a print shop. The salesman knew he had a hot one on the line when we came through the door, because Shorty started oohing and awing at the showroom Scout before us. I did my best as the younger brother who had been assigned the purchase price task. My brother was a Union truck driver and made good money, so all it took was a call to his banker and we drove home in his new Scout with a V8 engine. Mercy! Shorty was like a kid in the proverbial candy store. His first thought was to climb a mountain in four-wheel drive.

But, before we go there, I must tell you about this mountain of a man. When he was young, Mother said she thought he would never grow. He held that short stature until around twelve, and then the growth bean took off inside him. It didn't stop until he was 6'6" and weighed in at 250 pounds of rock-solid steel. His prowess at running and walking was unequaled in our family. His hunting and fishing abilities are legendary. He lived for the outdoors—a new pair of cowboy boots, some shotgun and rifle shells, a fly rod, and a place to use them all.

Beyond that, he was a favorite of everyone who knew him, a giant with a giant heart, filled with goodwill and laughter. He was just damned fun to be around! My other brothers and sister loved him as I did. He was open for the next big adventure when it came along, even if the adventure had some pitfalls involved.

In our youth, four-wheel drive vehicles were few and far between. My friends and I drooled over ads in the back of magazines telling us how to buy Army surplus Jeeps. It was all my buddies' dreams in high school. Our years of four-wheeling were in old Jeeps reclaimed by fathers who rebuilt them when they came home from war. Those old Jeeps hold some of my most sacred and scary memories as they rust out in someone's back field.

Two Scout adventures stand out among many in that rig, before he went on to his new Scout II. One winter elk hunt in Island Park, driving near where the power line now goes through, the snow was light and fluffy but slick on the shaded side hills, about eighteen inches deep. As we drove along looking for a place to disembark, we came around a steep side hill corner. The Scout started sliding sideways, down toward the ravine bottom. I yelled, "Stop!" And for once he did. We slid until a little tree saved the day. Shorty was sure backing up would clear us, no problem at all! Well, it didn't. After he had us well on our way to the bottom, Dad told him to put the brakes on and shut it down. A quick assessment of our situation told us we were in a hellava fix. The nearest anything was two miles back, it was 15 degrees, and afternoon was closing in. Dad didn't panic, he looked at us and said, "There's an old Cat back there on that log landing. I'm going back and try to crank it up." We sat there speechless, someone else's Caterpillar dozer and Dad was going to use it without permission! Off he went, while we all contemplated how we would trade off positions sleeping overnight in the Scout. When we heard that lumbering old Cat and its diesel rolling down the road, it was an auditory vision. He uncovered the old Cat, cranked its pony motor, and fired her up. It pulled us back up hill to solid footing, then Dad walked the Cat back and left a ten-dollar bill on the covered seat. He also left a note explaining his actions and his phone number. We never heard a word from the owner. Imagine that today!

Big Cottonwood Canyon, near Downey, was another of our favorite hunting grounds for mule deer. Known for its gumbo mud, when the rain came, you got the hell out of that canyon quickly. Coming out one night in a downpour, we rounded a corner and found the road blocked by a truck with two range riders and horses in the stock rack bed, all sliding down a hill, again stopped by a tree. Shorty decided he could pull them back up on the road. Before I could stop him, he had us latched onto the horse truck. The Scout could pull them back up all right, until it lost traction in the mud. The next move put us following the truck back down the hill, as the tow chain held tight. Another tree stopped the slide. The ensuing maneuvers saved the day. At my insistence, they chained the truck to a nearby pine, pulled the Scout toward the truck, loosened its tow chain, and we backed up onto the road. Hours later, with the help of other hunters and their chains, using Handyman jacks, sagebrush and log chunks, the truck, cowboys and horses, with rigging, made it out just before midnight.

Forty years later, we spoke of this on one of our last phone calls. He left us soon after, off on another Scout adventure memory and a smile in his heart.

L. Scott Hancock

# Wonderments

The winter blue of the Eastern Idaho sky is not a deep blue like that of Third Mesa turquoise in Arizona Hopi country. It ranges from opaque light blue to river blue as it breaks through the ice.

The sky was snowing ice crystals while I sipped my coffee this morning, trying to figure out where it was coming from. As I leaned in close to the nearest window and looked up to the top of our hundred-foot cottonwoods, the answer was evident. Fog had frozen to the limbs over the past very cold days and was still breaking loose as crystals fell from the top twenty feet of limbs (not yet heated by the sun) on the snow field below. It rained crystal flakes until sometime after the noon hour. What a splendid sight. It's these sorts of things folks who dislike snow and winter miss. I wouldn't trade winter for all the lower states' sunshine and lack of seasons. My broken-record statement is worth repeating: Winter gives us water!

While forming this story in my mind, other aspects became more important and the storyline took a quick left turn.

This morning, I was greeted with an email from Jerry Russell, a fellow writer for the *Island Park News*. He complimented me on a recent article and gave me his reasons for doing so. My day was made. Jerry is a gem. His articles give insights to readers, as his 90-plus years have given him wisdom from the ages. Jerry is as shiny as a new penny. Truly, when I met him, I would have aged him an early 70s man. His email awakened me, I needed to concentrate on how lucky we all are for having a voice in this wonderful, last-of-its-kind newspaper. And it's Editor Ann.

My fellow writers are genuine. The *I.P. News* is important for many reasons. My words and structure are inadequate to outline them. The paper gives voice to common folks, who have no other resource to represent them and what seems right. Past articles have addressed my admiration for Ken Watt's work, and my love of everything Wendy Pratt writes about her cattle, ranching, and good land stewardship. Others who write for the *News* are equal in measure. Jan Neish covers the theatrics of local politicians better than anyone I have read. Years ago, one of her articles explained the Idaho legislative session much better than any big city paper. It was brilliant.

Writers for the *I.P. News* share a commonality: a perspective that is theirs, not what they have been influenced to write. A talent apparent in the words of our beloved Elisa (E.C. Stilson) as she writes of others, her violin, and her daily journey with cancer. *Island Park News* articles are honest, not formulaic in structure or in compliance with self-anointed editors. This, in and of itself, is priceless in today's press, that follow themes of alignment with celebrity thinking. If you can subscribe, please do, to help guarantee real voices from real people. These outstanding gems of local journalism are disappearing rapidly. The remuneration for contributing writers is reader appreciation.

That said, let's move on. I found an actual value to my cell phone, other than its being yet another leash around my neck, pulling me back when I seek mindless freedom. Music is the answer I can come up with to assign worth to these denizens of evil. I can play my "halftime" music while I get dressed each morning. What the hell is halftime music, you ask? A lad in the distant past, who washed my windows and actually pumped my gas in Hayden Lake, Idaho, said to me one day as I listened to Mozart on my tape deck, "Boy, you sure do like that half-time music. You have a different one playing every time I pump your gas." When I questioned his meaning, he said, "You know, that kind of long-haired music they play during movie intermissions or at halftime." I took this as a compliment, as I never wanted to be an icon of sameness. Throw in a little Willie Nelson, Dolly Parton, or Judy Collins, and I'm your man.

Life is a constant battle between the relationships of forces for me. Recently I figured out the librarian at our house leaves a lot to be desired. Never one to write down the names of borrowers, books from our library are often lost to time and faceless readers who forget to return them. Prime example: I have tediously searched our shelves for a small book about Ray Lum. Ray was one of America's great characters, he bought and traded more mules and horses than any man in recorded history. Providing the government with mules for building the levees along the Mississippi, among other federal projects, he sold the cavalry their horses up through the 1930s. Known in twenty states as the most fair and honest mule trader. Ray's most famous quote was given in a Smithsonian journalist's interview, just before his death: "You live and you learn, then you die and forget it all." You might want to read a book about Ray, entitled *Ray Lum's Tales of Horses, Mules and Men.* Now, if someone out there knows the whereabouts of my Ray Lum book, please write. Library fines will not be assessed, but you will need to sign the borrower's book in the future before another volume leaves my shelves-if I can find the damn thing!

# Molly B'Damn and Wyatt

My mother was fascinated by the history of one of the West's most famous ladies of the night: Molly B'Damn, of Shoshone County fame, in the legendary town of Murray, Idaho. Mom would insist we take a trip up the Coeur d'Alene River to have a burger and beer at the Spragpole Bar and Museum, located just up the street from the Bedroom Mine Bar. It should be mentioned here my mother was not a drinker in any sense of the word, and would want the record to state this, but she loved the ice-cold mugs of beer served with a Spragpole burger. And she loved stories of Molly.

Maggie Hall (Molly B'Damn) was born in Dublin and came to America in her early twenties. She married a man who convinced her she could make more money selling her personal wares than any other venture. She prospered and left the husband for her chance at fame and fortune in the new gold strike area in the Coeur d'Alene mountains. She headed to this area up Prichard Creek after plying her wares in Oregon, California, and locales in Idaho.

Molly was quite well off at this juncture, with an incredible wardrobe for the period. On the pack trip into the gulch, heading up Pritchard Creek to the town of Murray, the group was overtaken by a horrible blizzard. Molly sent the pack string on for help and stayed behind building a temporary shelter for a young mother and child. She covered them in her expensive furs and huddled in the small shelter with her horse, keeping them from freezing for three days. When the rescue party returned, Molly was hailed as a hero in Murray, and her fame quickly spread to Spokane, Washington, and the newspapers.

Molly lived and worked in the area with her ladies until a smallpox epidemic pushed her into another heroic role. She organized the citizens to care for the ill and keep the town running. Her legend was expanded by her generosity. It was said Molly never turned away anyone who needed a meal or place to sleep. She worked the epidemic until he own health failed, and she died a hero's death in 1888.

Her story is still celebrated in Shoshone County each year with "Molly B'Damn Days." I couldn't tell you how many times I drove my mother to Molly's humble grave just outside Murray. Mom would sit and quietly stare and then comment on Molly's inherent goodness. Mother owned all the books about Molly and was her own Southeast Idaho historian on Molly's life.

The jury is still out on how much Wyatt Earp and his brother James interacted with Molly when the two Earp boys decided to engage in their never-ending search for striking it rich, which brought them to Murray, Idaho, in 1884. It has been rumored they admired Molly and her kindness to newcomers.

Wyatt and James set up shop just down the creek from Murray in Eagle, Idaho (not to be confused with the Eagle, near Boise). The Earps bought a giant circus tent and set up a saloon called the White Elephant. Their natural whiskey importing abilities, and the ladies they supplied made them wealthy for a while. But the trails into their area were limited and hard traveled, so Wyatt became a road builder up the gulches, and even served as a deputy sheriff for a time. When the cleared road trail was complete, he and his brother found other ventures in the West. The two of them left sometime in late 1884.

Wyatt had not completed one winter, leaving before the snow got so deep they would be stuck till spring. Molly knew the Earps, but to my knowledge no definitive history has been put forward as to what the relationship really was. Earp was later to claim they were partners after Molly's life became legend, the truth of which is open for speculation.

It all started up the river, when A.J. Pritchard discovered gold in the area in 1882. The gold and silver exploration in the area is well documented in any number of books. Gold-rich canyons of North Idaho played a significant role in the growth and wealth of early Spokane, Washington. This area of Shoshone County, Idaho, was rich with mining history and held potential fabulous wealth for the lucky prospector.

The tales are countless, from Noah Kellogg to the Lucky Friday, along with the Sunshine and Bunker Hill Mines, each with its own legends of the past, legends that bring thousands of visitors each year, to hear the voices of Molly and Wyatt echo through the gulches and river bottoms, stories of whiskey, miners, ladies of the night, and untold hardships.

Hopefully, these voices will forever whisper their stories on the wind and someday fill in the rest of the past and its secrets.

L. Scott Hancock

# Pump Handle and the Wagon

The prairies of Saskatchewan seemingly go on forever. Imagine what it seemed like in the early 1940s, to a boy living at the Canadian Pacific Depot in what he called Pump Handle, Saskatchewan. Truly out in the middle of nowhere, two real towns, Fife Lake and Cornach, were home to the best of the best in waterfowl hunting. The immense flyways for migratory birds made the United States flyways seem more like a flyby. The wheat and other grain fields ran for hundreds of miles, with the endless little pothole lakes that make the area perfect for northern nesting grounds, dreamland to grow up in and experience the real earth essence of life, values that are being bludgeoned out of us daily, by television and other media nonsense.

As my friend Dennis says, "Learning today lacks texture." How true! When kids, we had the opportunity to be outside making our own fun, getting dirty and playing games that today's societal ninnies would go apoplectic over. Especially if they knew the lack of barriers we had in garnering life's full experiences, good, and bad. We learned firsthand. We learned not to jump off cliffs because our friends dared us. We learned how to fend for ourselves in daily encounters that came along as part of our living routine.

My friend Jim grew up in this open-ended Saskatchewan wonderment, after a rough go with German measles. We talked about his story recently because it fascinates me no end, especially in light of today's health care being guided by insurance providers, pharmaceuticals and corporate medical hacks, that only see the next pill or injection as the answer. Healing in great part, comes from within.

As Jim lost most of his former weight, his mother and the town doctor grew more concerned. Rightly so. German measles killed thousands of people worldwide. The Canadian prairie was no exception. When he got out of bed, his mother wrapped his jeans around him, safety pinned on the side to tighten the grip on his nonexistent hips. The getting-up trips grew less and less.

His father was a station master and telegrapher for the Canadian Pacific Railroad. The family lived in a Canadian Pacific Depot. Jim's bedroom looked out on the board deck of the loading platform, used for passengers and freight. As he grew weaker, those around him feared recovery was not going to come about.

Each day he gazed out onto the railroad platform and beyond to the horizon, too young to realize how ill he really was. Awakening one morning, his eyes took him out to the train landing. In front of his window was a new wooden wagon.

In a recent phone call, Jim said, "Can you imagine being out on the Saskatchewan prairie in a rural train station, peering out your window and seeing a brand-new wagon?" As a matter of fact, I could. When I was in the polio hospitals in the 1950s, I witnessed near miracles of like nature with fellow patients.

As the days wore on, the wagon got rained and snowed on, and his desire to play with it grew. His recall of how he got out to the platform and the wagon is vague, but he did. He credits the wagon for his healing to this day. Each day, he pulled himself up and out to the plank station platform, pulling his wagon and gaining strength. His father overlooked the near-death sentence everyone else gave him, and decided a child's mind could and would respond to a greater stimulus than medicine. The wagon was the stimulus he needed!

I received photos recently of the train station in Pump Handle and of Jim's father with buddies after a duck hunt. One photo shows his father dressed up in front of a chalkboard on the station wall, with times and destinations handwritten in appropriate squares. Behind his father, one frame shows the time it takes to arrive in Moose Jaw.

Jim, long removed from Pump Handle, his mother's one-room school house teaching assignments, and his father's station master days, said the story of his wagon and road back to health remained a solid conviction in his mind. I have no doubt of the wagon's elixir of magic in leading to his recovery.

There is much to be learned from stories like these that inspire and move us to greater attainment! We need to believe in our inherent health, not the ill health we are reminded of hourly on television and other media propaganda outlets.

# Truefitt & Hill, Est. 1805

This morning, while shaving, tragedy came to visit me and my long-serving, soft and pliable shaving brush. It broke at the bindings in the handle, and bristles started to fall out in the sink. Its time had come after twenty-four years of noble and daily service.

Think of how many shaves it had spread lather on my face, while a Liszt piano piece played in the background. I witnessed the cracks in the handle some time ago, but like an old friend with a limp, you always hope for the best. The cracks got worse, until this morning's breakage completed the service record of this old friend.

It ended on a good note, however. I had just completed my warm water shave using Truefitt & Hill mug shaving soap. Nothing is as lovely as this wonderful old cream. It has been with the British, long serving the Empire before the times of Lord Kitchener of Khartoum.

We know for a fact Kitchener and Winston Churchill enjoyed this rich lather each morning with their first brandy. Truefitt's was made an official supplier to the Crown's service by the first Duke of Edinburgh. Yes, I still shave with an antiquated safety razor, that has been difficult to restore blades in the battery because of its lack of popularity in this mindless, use it, and throw it away culture, a culture that then moves on rapidly to the next bit of nonsense.

Not long ago, I feared I was running short on razor cartridges, so my wife ordered more, though they be aftermarket items. Upon their arrival, when putting them away, she discovered that I had quite an abundance in the back of the storage drawer. Good! I think now I can shave with recognized comfort until I take the final rest below the daisies.

Other shave lathers grace my face on occasion, including a fine canned foam from England, with a nice sandalwood fragrance. But in truth, my almost daily use is still Williams cake soap. It lathers beautifully and is environmentally perfect, coming in a small cardboard box easy to dispose of. It remains one of the great product buys of today.

But the problem remained—what to do about the broken shave brush? Yes, I had plenty of others, but as I looked them over, none could be pressed into service because they were antique, pure boar bristle brushes made long ago. Different friends had found them at garage sales, and my wife, who left us a few years back, spoiled me with some fine European masterpieces.

Hearing of my problem and understanding my eccentricities, Colleen, my darling, guiding, indulging spouse, went searching in my bathroom drawers, finding a nice brush I had in storage for just such a time when I faced shaving disaster. It's a dandy, however I'm not sure it will be used. It too is a pure boar bristle brush, given to me by someone who knew of my love for good shaving support items.

What is a boar bristle brush? Exactly as it sounds, a brush whose hairs are pure bristle hairs from a boar pig. Originally made from European wild boar, now they are primarily scraped from domestic swine after they have been dispatched just before butchering. They make the finest brushes, bar none.

Pat, my beloved sister-in-law from Great Britain, who lives on a quiet hill in the Napa Valley of California, listens to my stories of Churchill and once produced a photograph of her father and Churchill together for me to admire. She too indulges my odd whims, and in the past has shared some of her Crown Cutlery with me to admire over a lovely dinner. She would approve, I'm sure, of my Truefitt & Hill, Ultimate Comfort Shaving Cream.

When one uses Truefitt, the brush is dampened ever so lightly, because the cream makes lather on your face with a tiny bit of moisture. This is why it was used in the dry areas of the British Empire during the colonial period. Where water was sparse, Truefitt was the ticket for shaving! Used in the Sudan and other areas of Africa, it use was widespread as the tub containing the cream had a tightly screwed-on lid, as it does to this day. Therefore, a dab could be placed on the brush, the lid replaced quickly, and the cream saved from drying up.

I was first introduced to fine shaving lathers by my departed Swiss wife, who found Truefitt and gave me my first experience in face luxury for Christmas one year. I saved the empty tub for years, and when she left us, I used it to send part of her ashes to family in Switzerland, there to be placed in the forest her beloved Rudi and Heidi owned. It was a noble end for a Truefitt jar.

And now, for an admission to my nephew Randy: Yes, I used the word 'eccentric.'

I hope you are pleased as to my admission.

# Now, it's Fall

More than twenty pumpkins have been gleaned from the garden. Boxes of tomatoes have been given to all who wanted them. The 91-year-old man on Meridian Street has his apples bagged from his historic orchard, waiting for buyers to come along and drop five dollars into the can when a bag is taken home. All is right with the world in Blackfoot.

With most of the potato harvest behind them, the beet farmers are moving quickly to get their crop out of the ground and to the beet dumps, waiting to be shipped off and processed before hard winter. The days are shorter but still wonderfully warm, the overnight frosts are yet mild. Our yard is a carpet of leaves, with at least a couple more inches to come when the final installments are released from their branch holdings.

For those who have read my works before, you understand that fall is my year-end and beginning, not January. The pattern was set in youth, I guess. The best fishing, and, of course, hunting began when the branches started to bare and the sunlight turned more golden all day long.

Yesterday, I went to an 11-year-old girl's birthday party in Shelley. A wonderful young lady named Emma, whom I have written about before when she passed her hunter safety course, and later we went shooting in the desert. Emma now has a hunting bow, and if she is as good with it as she is with a rifle all will be well as she goes afield.

My fall begins when the elk start bugling in the high country, sometimes as early as late August up north. In the early years, when I was a lot more Skookum, I would sit on a meadow edge in Island Park, waiting as Dad and my brothers moved off to the dark woods and started their slow walking hunt. As the sun rose in that cold country, the layers of clothes would be shed, and as daylight came along, I would be treated to magnificent awakenings, like the Tetons right in front of me outlined in pre-dawn black.

The outdoors should never simply be about the harvest, but moreover about just being there, and what it can give you spiritually. Dad said the outdoors was his church, and I have tried to make it mine; what grander cathedral can there be?

So many great writers have spoken of the fall in their words, I can't possibly improve on their observations. But I can say this time of year makes my blood run a bit faster as I see a rooster take wing, or a mule deer buck run across an aspen-choked meadow and into the thick jack pine woods near the mouth of a ravine.

Both fields that border our property have been harvested of their barley crop, and the Canada geese have moved in to nibble on the winter wheat coming up already, where the barley stood a month ago.

Nephew Kent and his son, Chris, have been to the upper reaches of the Blackfoot Reservoir, near the Wyoming line, on an early goose hunt, and scouting the range for their elk hunt, which begins soon. The mandated reclaim of the land there, after it has been mined, is almost unbelievable. I could not see or have known a mining project had removed tons and tons of ore had I not been told. The elk have prospered in that reclaimed environment, with all the new trees and grasslands that were planted back as the mining ended. They number in the thousands in that area near Soda Springs. Good for them, and good for us. When I was a kid, those mining operations near Soda left a great, ugly gash in the earth.

Things change, and not always as we expect or are told. I have a book on mule deer that has been around thirty years or so. This book speaks of the demise of mule deer, as they are not as adaptable as white-tailed deer. How wrong the book was! Now, the muleys have become so habituated they inhabit parks and lawns across many towns in their range. Some towns have had to resort to scare tactics to stop them from wandering downtown city streets. On a recent visit to our beloved Elisa, who writes for the *Island Park News*, I almost ran into two mule deer walking down her street in the Pocatello suburbs.

Wild turkeys are so abundant now in North Idaho I had to shoo them off my front porch railings, so guests didn't have to step carefully over their leavings. They roosted in our evergreens by the dozens at night. Turkeys have been introduced and thrived so well, they even roam the streets of cities like Spokane. Again in Pocatello, I ran into a flock of wild turkeys on Mohawk Drive, which seems appropriate to the name. In both cases, as with most wild animals, fall is the time to store the last layer of body fat to withstand the bitter cold months to come.

In the fall, with the wind literally blowing away their cover, the wild of things becomes more easily seen and marveled at. Maybe that's just one more reason I love this time of year. Warm your heart in the fall sun as it lowers to the horizon.

Photo: Mule deer buck in my nephew's garden, Pocatello.

L. Scott Hancock

# Rest in Peace

A line from a Hemingway tribute ran through my mind as I looked up to the tops of the cottonwoods, towering eighty feet or more above me. "The high blue windless skies" kept repeating in my subconscious, as I heard the real words of those gathered to memorialize a woman who had left us in April. This past Saturday up Indian Creek, south of Pocatello, was chosen as the time we could all meet and talk lovingly about the lady who had left us. My opening prayer, requested by the family, was difficult in the sense that I had to leave out so much that needed to be said. It didn't matter, as most in attendance knew the left out parts.

I had known this woman since childhood, as we had all come from the same neighborhood, and she was my cousin's close friend. After college and moving to North Idaho, I lost track of her until I heard she was marrying my nephew's brother-in-law. This made me happy as I knew he was a stellar man, with a loving, kind heart, the kind of man she so richly deserved, and needed, for her life to gain a normality she had not known.

As I waited under the apple tree, listening to different people tell their stories of how she touched their lives, my mind went back to a dark tool shed, a lightning storm with tremendous thunder, and a loss of power. My uncle had yelled from the house for us to stay in the shed until the storm passed. What was a great excitement to my cousin and me was terror for her when the power went out. She started crying and shaking in panic and fear. To a boy of eleven, it was an adventure; to her, it was a nightmare. As the lightning crashed around us, her shaking increased. I put my arm around her shoulder and told her everything would be okay, the storm would be gone soon. From the silence of the darkened shed she said, "I hate my life."

I haven't the words, all these years later, to express how this statement affected me. I later heard from my cousin that she hated life because of her mother and her mother's boyfriends. Some days later my father asked me why I was not paying attention to a job we were doing, so I told him the story, and what my cousin had said about the adult men in our friend's life. Dad turned ashen and went into the house. I later heard in passing that the police had investigated and found no issues. Soon after, this girl was sent off to an orphanage on a train by herself.

I knew none of this until her daughter and granddaughter came to my home after her death, to hear my story and about our childhood together. Her dear husband came along, as he knew many of the stories and tried every way he could to heal the wounds. But the demons and ghosts were with her till the end. The lack of trust and grounding followed her throughout her life. This emptiness kept her away from the common daily enjoyments we all find so natural. She loved and gave freely of her heart to her children and others, but inevitably the past would return, and she had no way to understand it, and draw from its security and comfort. Her life was filled with moves, as houses she lived in became 'haunted'. Her fears would overcome all logic when confronted with a life happening she could not fathom. And all the while, this good person tried her best to cope with the unknown.

The cottonwoods above my head moved slowly as I remembered another time on Indian Creek, so long ago when I took a grand mule deer buck. The folks speaking of her in the background drew me back to the present. I listened and wondered how much they really knew about this lady, who had been locked in closets and abused in horrible ways. Ways that never left the adult, and yet nothing was done by the authorities in the late 1950s to bring justice to her tormented life!

Dad spoke of another man whom he and others suspected of child sexual abuse. My mother was mortified, as the man in question was a pillar of respectability in his church and political community. After Dad's death, the truth came out, and Mother felt terrible she had not listened to my father. How many lives had this community leader ruined?

The apple trees and aspens rustled with a newfound breeze as we ate our memorial dinner, and the guests visited in the shade. My heart was full as I prayed this dear lady finally found peace and contentment in a world of serenity and calm. She brought beauty to so many she loved, even in view of her own, sometimes tragic, life! May you rest in peace. Love, Scott.

# Story Time

When I saw Pam standing at the counter of my favorite sports shop in Sandpoint, Idaho, she seemed distressed. My dear friend, Mr. Raiha, looked at me, then said to her, "I bet Scott can fix it, or tell you of someone who can." It was early spring in North Idaho. The snowpack was heavy, and when the thaw came with torrential rains, it caused the usual gravel road washouts. Pam was the wife of Mark Story, a well-known TV industry creator/director and photographer of legendary commercials. I had acquaintance with the Storys through mutual friends, but we were on a howdy basis only, when we met at the store or post office in our small town of Hope.

Pam looked at me in desperation, asking if I would look at her road and advise as to repairs. When I arrived on their side of the hill above our beautiful little town, the roadway up the steep grade was channels, forced by melting snow and coastal-like rain, building runoff in river-sized proportions. The ruts were fourteen inches deep and barely passable. When I finished my evaluation, Pam and I spoke on the phone. She was flying back to Canada, to help Mark with a new commercial in the midst of filming. My confidence in a solution to her problem gave her a break from 'road agony,' as she called it. "I'll have Mark call you with his go-ahead or denial."

Late that evening, a phone call came in from Montreal, Canada, where Mark was filming a commercial. He was as blunt as a pickaxe, asking if I felt confident in fixing the road correctly so washouts would never repeat again. I assured him if it failed after my corrected repair, I would reimburse him the roadwork expenditure. It was the beginning of a long relationship.

I moved in a heavy front-end loader and peeled the roadway back, added filter fabric, and repaved with compacted aggregate, then rolled the road for two days employing a massive road roller. All ended well. Needless to say, the road is still there in perfect condition twenty-five years later.

"Pizza, Pizza" was the joke around the job. It was one of Mark's famous lines from a commercial he created for a major pizza company.

Mark was once described to me by an internationally famous artist as "world-class eccentric." He hit the mark, so to speak. Storyville, as my employees called it, encompassed 160 acres of buildings and grounds that rivaled something one would see in an old-world country. Beautiful and singular, with one magnificent property attraction after the other around each corner.

My work at Storyville was broad with multiple projects, including the creation of barrier walls to retard mountain runoff from flooding the wine cellar, where it could ruin thousands of dollars of collectable vintage wines. Also, on this project we waterproofed the 100-yard underground shooting range. The workmen assembled new rock paths around the property leading to the greenhouse, photo studio and other specific purpose structures. One project, a staggering koi pond for his fish, some as expensive as a car! I designed, and the boys built, a series of waterfalls over huge flat rocks. The water fell evenly, resembling an Appalachian stream over slab granite. Mark, upon seeing it on a return trip from Switzerland, said, "I have seen these all over the world, and this is the best."

The list goes on, but one is of singular importance. He wanted to have a wide patio deck built off the back of a tiny ledge that surrounded the rear of his house. A difficult problem to overcome was a rock cliff that fell straight down for about twenty feet. Countless sketches later, and a pile of research, I came up with structural pipe we could core drill into the mountain rock and build up from there.

As if that wasn't enough, he also requested an infinity pool that fell off into space, with Lake Pend Oreille as a backdrop. I hired more and more men, with my lead carpenter, Jim Ford, heading the charge. While the pipes were being cemented into the hillside after core drilling, and the structural welding in progress, I drove to Boise. I enlisted a fiberglass genius who could build the pools to be placed into the deck, creating a knife-edge of water spilling over then being caught in a catch basin ten feet below. The water was then pumped back up continuously, keeping the pool depth level perfect. The deck, with the infinity pool, grew to over 70-feet long, with a supporting pump and control room below. During this process, we also built a new deck on the front of his lap pool swimming building. The building had a garage-type door that, when lifted, brought in the outdoors, instilling the image of swimming toward the lake hundreds of feet below.

On one occasion, Mark frowned at the meals the men were eating for lunch. "I want you to get a caterer to bring good food and lemonade here each day at noon." I did so, which made a local restaurateur very happy. Another time, he walked through the project asking how much each man made. He then told me how much to raise their individual hourly wage.

Mark was often hard to please, obtuse, but always fair. He completed two famous photography books after semi-retiring, covering people born in three different centuries. A marvelous photographer and television director, capping off an illustrious career. His talent was monumental in various forms. The

Internet has lots of Mark Story stories. It was one of my life's great blessings to be able to work at Storyville. Mark sold his mountain retreat and left North Idaho not long before I pulled up stakes. The stampede of newcomers, lured by inexpensive city life, sadly changed the quiet, engaging lifestyle forever.

Photos: Me in front of the infinity pool and deck system.

# One of A Kind

Some years back I received a postcard from South America, sent from a friend who had worked for me. He was on an adventure with his father, riding the ridges of the Andes on off-road motorcycles. Amazing as it was, it was not amazing for Kip or his renowned world-class adventurer dad, Royal Shields.

This is not a story of one of my intimates. Royal and I were friends, but not day-to-day-contact friends as so many people are. My first contact with Royal was forgotten until he reminded me. As told by him, "You were sitting on a deer stand hunting in Priest Lake, when I spied you with binoculars." Seeing my wheelchair outline, he decided to come over and meet me.

From there, we crossed paths from time to time until one day he called and asked if I would be interested in building his mother's new house on a hill in Hope, Idaho. Royal was a long-time architect from Sandpoint, and I knew he had a reputation as an explorer and wild man adventure seeker, which led to his legend status, obtained by those who knew of his feats. He lived on the edge!

Whenever the subject came up of someone's wild experiences in the outdoors, Royal's name and his like adventure was used as a point of reference for comparison. And in the same breath, these words would be added: "I have no doubt one day I'll open the paper and his name will appear as a headline, describing how he met his end skiing over an avalanche ridge line, or some similar daring-do."

To know Royal was to know a mild-mannered man, so humble and unassuming one would think he was the librarian at the local grade school. To hear his voice, you had to lean in as he spoke so mildly with soft tones and rounded words. I doubt he ever raised his voice, except in hollering for a lost son, wife, or companion on one of his open-ended treks. Where he went, his sons, Fremont and Kip, would follow if allowed, with Jana, his wife, in tow, if time and good sense permitted.

Royal lived for the outdoors and the next path untaken, or any challenge therein he deemed interesting enough to pursue. These pursuits often brought him home late, wet, cold, exhilarated, exhausted, and joyous. The very next morning, he would kayak to work across the bay, by the Long Bridge in Sandpoint, to his architectural office. He commuted by boat on any but the worst weather days.

Carpenters who worked on the Bavarian-style compound on the Hope Peninsula told the story of Royal consulting on the site, and future direction of the work to be done, then jumping into a twelve-foot boat with a small motor and heading out across icy Lake Pend Oreille after dark, to return home miles away. When I told him about this, he responded, "When I hit an ice floe, I would open up the throttle on the boat motor, hit the floe and skip up on it, hoping I had enough speed to skid me to the other side and open water."

His off-road motorcycling was a boon to hikers. He would take chainsaws and axes with him, and clear trails to the top of places like Wellington Peak near Hope. Some trails cleared by the Forest Service, he complained about, as he wanted them left primitive.

I don't think the word "tough" is adequate for Royal. Indomitable and prepared, like an accomplished Boy Scout, he could withstand (and often did) nights under a tree, isolated by a sudden blizzard, or in pursuit of a buck he saw as the light dimmed to darkness.

His needs were simple, and he would eat anything. As our mutual friend Kevin said when we spoke of Royal recently, "Royal could survive anywhere. Hell, he would eat sticks if he had to." I know this to be true. He and I would snack on some pretty weird food choices when he came to consult on one of my projects.

He travelled the world in his quests of hunting, fishing, or just exploring. He once showed me a photo of a massive grizzly paw outline, next to his shoe print of the night before, while hiking in the Yukon.

Royal stories could fill an entire day around a campfire. They will be met and expanded on by two outstanding sons who share the spirit, their offspring, and Jana, with all her adventures beside Royal, most knew nothing of. To that point, Royal never sought the limelight; in fact, he fled from it as an intensely private man. Few in the general public were aware of his other worlds, besides architecture.

Modest, humble, talented, unassuming, generous of heart and effort, he died two weeks ago while driving to pick up a bicycle rider in distress. The bike race was sponsored by his Rotary International Club in Sandpoint. As a 45-year member, he quietly supported the community in Rotary and other civic organizations. No fanfare in death; his heart gave out. An exit not perfect in its timing, which leaves a giant hole to fill, in the wild of things. And in our need for "outsiders," who are like a line from a poem by Robert Service: "A race of men who don't fit in, a race that can't be still."

Royal will not soon be duplicated, but the family will produce another hiker to the heavens with joy in their soul, and a one-of-a-kind smile on their face. Royal was an Iron Man long before it became Yuppie fashionable. This quote from his obituary is perfect: "In the end, we all become stories."

# "Rhythm of the Rails"

Pocatello Creek Canyon, as it narrowed just beyond the East Terry Street turnoff returning to downtown, was a series of beautiful little farms in my youth. Just up the canyon, gaining elevation at each turn, Hobe Hall, a retired trainman, slept lazily on his front porch in a big easy chair, placed there for just such purpose. We had made the monthly trip for Dad to give Hobe another payment on Hobe's retired 1936 Hamilton Railroad watch, purchased on a 'pay as pay can' plan between Dad and Hobe.

The watch, I own to this day, runs perfectly after it was finally fixed by a young man in Sandpoint. Jason was truly the best-trained watch repairman I have encountered. Unfortunately, his clock and watch repair shop in the Old Ninth Grade Center in Sandpoint was short-lived because of a lack of appreciation for quality fine old timepieces. Today, we view digital junk!

Hobe was very old when I was very young. He had experiences on the Union Pacific that should have been documented for the ages. Alas, so many of these oral histories have gone to the heap of missed opportunities. Dad bought the watch to help out an old retiree, living on a modest pension in those days.

Hobe had a story for me on each visit. His stories of being a brakeman and fireman on the Union Pacific Railroad included a stint working in Ogden, Utah, behind the magnificent Big Boy locomotive. When he would commence his stories about the

Big Boy, and his role in making runs from Ogden to Cheyenne, Wyoming, I was enthralled.

Big Boy was an unrealized dream to me. The immensity of this behemoth locomotive was a thrill to a young rail nut's mind. The Ogden grade in Utah required helper locomotives to pull the long ore trains coming out of Wyoming. This was a costly difficulty for Union Pacific. In the early 1940s, U.P. gave an order to Schenectady Locomotive Works in New York to design and build a locomotive that could pull the heavy, long train ore cars over the Ogden grade without the help of helpers. The birth of the Big Boy was the perfect solution to an annoying problem. Big Boy garnered enough power needed to do the job in one locomotive.

In 1941, Union Pacific took delivery of the first of twenty-seven units built. Weighing in at 1.2 million pounds, with over 636,000 pounds of tractive power, Big Boy could pull a small town had it been on wheels. One hundred thirteen feet long, creating vibrations as it passed that shook houses in small towns, like Kemmerer, Wyoming, on its ore runs.

Hobe would regale me with memories of blizzards out on the Wyoming plains, with ore cars behind Big Boy for as long as you could see, and that massive steam wonderment pulling all those cars while plowing through snow drifts four and five feet deep. He said, "On many occasions we prayed to make it through the winter maelstroms and arrive at the next depot, and to waiting hot coffee."

Hobe's watch has all the markings inside where it was engraved by certified railroad jewelers, including one in Cheyenne. The date of the watch being set is clear on the inside of the back cap, completing this glorious piece of history. Keep in mind, railroads in that era had absolute rules about punctuality, another habit lost today in this new era of 'I'll get to it when I can' attitude.

Eventually, Big Boy locomotives were replaced by diesel/electric units, and these leviathans were retired to various scrap yards and railroad parks for viewing across the United States. One engine, Number 4014, was brought back to Cheyenne from California to be refurbished, so once again it could celebrate the glory of the heyday of steam locomotives using diesel/electric power instead of coal. 4014 was present at the celebration to commemorate the 150$^{th}$ anniversary of the driving of the Golden Spike, at Promontory Point in Utah.

This year, Number 4014 will come West again, stopping at a variety of depots in towns frequented during the height of steam power in America. I will be in my hometown to welcome it back! Some of my readers may remember a story I wrote, speaking of a once-in-a-lifetime opportunity to ride behind my Uncle Ren Poulson while he engineered one of the last of these giants to Ogden, the grand machine then traveling onto Cheyenne for retirement, a permission the railroads would go apoplectic about today, with their lawyers and liability. But the superintendent of the Pocatello Yards gave his approval to the 'nutty kid in the wheelchair.'

One of the finest benefits of my using a wheelchair was that trip. Big Boy rocked and clanged all the way to Ogden, the noise deafening and the smoke outside blinding the view of the passing landscape. I registered every moment of that ride, reliving it in my mind to this day.

In the audience at the Union Pacific depot in Pocatello when Big Boy comes to town again, I will be smiling and telling anyone who wants to hear about my voyage inside that monstrous powerhouse of steam-driven glory. Just to hear the steam whistle will raise hairs on your neck. You can do so on

YouTube, by typing in the words "Big Boy." Seeing it in person is a sight you will never regret! I promise you.

# Poky and the Iron Road

Just before I left Bonner County, to come back to my home country to "be old," I wrote a letter to the local paper outlining the faulty sentiment that the railroad was a huge hazard to Lake Pend Oreille.

The new nonsensical folks that had moved in wanted the railroad gone. I supported wholeheartedly the proposed railroad bridge span crossing near the old 1905 bridge, to avoid the very lake pollution they feared, should a train derail into the lake. As people are fond of quoting now, "It's not rocket science." The most important aspect to counter the environmentalists who hated the railroad was this: to transport what one train engine and 36 flatcars could over 500 miles, it would take four times the semi-trucks and hundreds more gallons of diesel. Trains still are the most economical form of mass product transport, period!

Unabashedly, I admit I am a train addict. Forgive me this sin against organic thought, but I was raised in a railroad town. I grew up with folks who made a good living and have great retirements from the railroad, honest, hardworking railroaders who were proud of their livelihood, and wore the caps and engineer bib overalls of the Union Pacific in Pocatello.

The railroad built Pocatello (Poky, as natives call it). It all started in 1845 with a man named Asa Whitney, who petitioned Congress to enact legislation for the westward expansion of the railroads. Pocatello became a city in 1882 or '89 (argument exists here) with the railroad its grandest employer, paying good wages and providing housing that could be purchased reasonably by its workers. Located where the mountains opened up to the Snake River Plain at the Portneuf Gap, the railroad beds followed the old wagon trails to Oregon and to Fort Hall, a main trading post in the early westward expansion.

The original Utah and Northern railroads were promoted by John W. Young, a son of the president of the Mormon Church. Eventually, consolidation brought in the Oregon Short Line, and ultimately, all were bought out by the Union Pacific Railroad Company.

Poky was the largest division point west of Omaha, with tracks running south, north, east, and west. During its heyday, in the late '50s, dozens of trains ran through Union Pacific rail yards each day. Imagine the delight of disembarking in Pocatello's beautiful depot, then walking to any number of local grand hotels like the Yellowstone, Whitman, or the cream of the crop, the Bannock. The Bannock was so fancy that, as my friend Helen from Sandpoint said, "The waiters wore white gloves, as I recall." Indeed, they did. My brothers worked at all three of these grand old hotels, all of which still stand except the Bannock.

The round house at Poky was the largest on the western line and could reverse the direction of a locomotive on its huge turntable. The location of this large rail yard gave it strategic value during World War II. The trains were the only form of transport heavy enough to haul Navy battleship gun barrels inland, for refurbishing at Pocatello's Naval Ordinance Plant. The N.O.P. employed hundreds of workers and still stands today. If you ever visit a World War II battleship at berth in a harbor, keep in mind its deck guns were probably relined in Pocatello. Far enough inland that enemy bombers would have a hard time reaching it, the plant remains today, in other usage. All because of the railroad.

My father was a journeyman boiler maker at the yards in Pocatello. They built and refurbished boilers on steam locomotives from around the West in the Pocatello shops. In 1954, over four hundred boiler makers were laid off with the advent of diesel/electric locomotives. Some workers were called back to different jobs on the line. My dad couldn't afford to hold out, so he went to work for the county. So many workers were laid off nationwide that Congress finally addressed the issue with railroad retirement legislation. The Railroad Retirement Act outlined the number of years one needed to work to receive at least a partial pension. It saved my parents and thousands of others by giving them retirement benefits they had earned but were denied before this law came into being.

I had so many relatives that worked for the railroad I couldn't name them all. My Uncle Ren (Christian) Poulson was a legend, written about in many history books. He ran a mule engine, hauling concrete for the American Falls Dam, when he was fifteen. He retired fifty-plus years later, and just before retirement, he engineered a locomotive to its last location, on display in Ross Park. My dad made the last side sheets for the boiler on that locomotive.

Uncle Ren arranged for me to ride with him to Ogden on a Big Boy locomotive, as a treat before his retirement. I loved the Big Boy and knew its history intimately. The U.P. yard superintendent was a member of the Elks Lodge, as were my uncles. He had heard of my love of trains and gave his permission. I remember to this day being lifted up into the cab, my crutches and leg braces banging as I sat down next to Dad.

Oh my god, I was in Heaven! The Big Boy was the largest locomotive ever built for Union Pacific, with 689,000 pounds of tractive power. Big Boy was over 85 feet long and weighed well over one million pounds. Recently, Union Pacific sent a Big Boy to the anniversary event at Promontory Point in Utah. Refurbished, it is now powered by diesel/electric but still gives a thrill to feel the ground shake as she roars by, 500 tons of rolling steel magnificence. I suggest reading *Hear the Lonesome Whistle Blow* by Dee Brown for an interesting start to railroad history.

# Trees and Other Friends

Yesterday, when my phone rang, I was outside looking up at the clouds, trying to formulate my next column for the *Island Park News*. Serendipitously, my thoughts were completed about the column as the call ended. Not the idea I had in mind, but a more beautiful creation was spawned.

My old, dear friend Jim, the mechanic, called from his new house up the Yaak River in northwestern Montana, near the Idaho border. Jim, like so many others I know, has left the Sandpoint area after years of doing business there, to seek peace and meaning no longer extant in that part of Bonner County. Sad, but ever so true, third and fourth generation Bonner County families are moving on. They realize the county is now so overrun by carpetbaggers and newbies, with millions in their pockets, life is never going to be a slow pace again.

"Scott, the tamaracks here are just unbelievable. The mountains are covered with them, all gold and orange, and I am sitting here in the fall sunshine at 65 degrees. This is paradise." As he went on, my mind envisioned the tamaracks (really, western larch) and the gold hillsides of fall, as they lose their needles annually but give a resplendent display before looking naked and bare, like a Charlie Brown Christmas tree, until the next spring. Many is the newcomer who asks, "What kind of disease is killing all those trees on the hillsides?"

Jim has found a new home, and my heart feels good about his new digs. He is just a short crow flight from the home of Tom Oar and his wife, Nancy, who have gained fame from the TV show *Mountain Men*. If you have seen the program, you soon realize the Oars are the real deal. They have lived up the Yaak, trapping and doing native craft arts for over forty-five years. Both are warm and inviting folks who show us how to do lost crafts of heritage woodsmen and Native Americans with humor, talent, and grace.

Still sleeping in his camper, Jim hasn't found the right mattress for his house bed and hasn't set up his woodshop to do minor alterations on his sleep platform. On top of that, he can't receive mail at his house because he has not yet made the mailbox. He's that kind of guy—a craftsman of unbelievable skill with mechanics or any task he chooses to take on. I won't be surprised if he is in his camper until the snow flies. He is so appreciative of his new house; he'll wait till the new wears off in his mind.

Jim lived above his auto shop for over twenty-five years, in pretty spare surrounds. This new opulence has him overwhelmed. He went on to tell me about the small pond across the road, and the neighbors who share his idea of the good life. The Yaak River Valley is amazing, uninhabited for the most part. You drive thirty-five miles up before you come across the bar and last outpost of what we term civilization. Grizzlies and wolves are prevalent, along with folks who just want woods living, and simple pleasures. Jim said another old friend who came to visit him remarked, "Jim, the air's so pure here it must have just come from the tap." Gotta love it!

That line reminded me of another old timer's quotes. My old pal, Lon, who was raised in the same neck of the woods but on the Idaho side, had some dandies.

Lon was a true string bean- he was tall, thin as a rail, and real. When a mutual friend died, Lon told me, "Ya know, Scott, he just woke up dead." Or when he wanted me to visualize what he was trying to describe, he would say, "Now, Scott, picturize this in your head." Another Lon classic came when he would tell me about good firewood and what not to use: "Ya know Scott, that damned pine burns too quick, and you don't get much 'buts' out of it." The first time I heard this one, it took a minute to realize he was talking about BTUs. He preferred buckskin tamarack that had lots of 'buts' for every chunk of wood put in the stove."

Lon was so tall and thin, the old timers at Hazy's Chevron station in Clark Fork said, "When Ol' Lon dies, we're going to put him in a fly pole carrying case and stand him up in a post hole; saves on ground space in the cemetery." We need more of these colorful characters in this speeding, crazy world of nonsense celebrities and other narcissistic transplant fools, flooding into Idaho's Panhandle.

My last article in *I P News* talked, in part, about fly fishing in Island Park. When my cousin heard of it, he said on the phone, "Remember when our dads fished there, wading those icy waters in their bib overalls?" Yes, I remembered, and wrote about that very thing. I hope to think about it until my own sunset comes, when I dream fishing dreams of Island Park and the magic waters of the Yellowstone country in Eastern Idaho.

*L. Scott Hancock*

# Red Wings and Spring

Time and calendars have rarely worked for me. They mark the beginning or ending of things that have been identified as boundaries to be observed; therefore, they have never set well with my own frameworks of allotted time spans that outline my world. As I grow older and more obtuse in thought, the clarity of my own world operation seems quite normal.

Spring has come in with the Red Winged Blackbirds, for as long as I can recall in my rhythm calendar world. Two arrived a week ago, and today the flock has taken over the bird feeders. Red Wings are among my favorite birds. The song they sing as they trill from the cattails and bulrushes is a sound once heard, brings memories of where you were when you first heard it.

Years ago, I lived just across the road from the boat ramp on upper Twin Lakes in North Idaho. Around this boat ramp were two old cabins that were used part of the year but remained uninhabited and silent over winter. Their yards, come true spring, would be inundated with Red Wings waiting for the snow to abate on the marshes at the lake's headwaters flowing down from runoff on Mount Spokane. Hundreds of Red Wings would sing all day long, making music that was soothing and stimulating at the same time. I wrote a poem about it, long forgotten, and probably best it is.

With the Red Wings come my brother's and Payson's birthdate. My brother left us some years ago, but Payson, my beloved little buddy who made fishing lures with me, doesn't let me forget his special day. He called me two weeks ago and asked if I would come to dinner with his family at his favorite restaurant in Idaho Falls. Writing about Payson and his obsession with fishing was one of the first articles I wrote for the *Blackfoot Morning News*. He later was featured in an article that appeared in my book, titled "Wall Hangers and New Beginnings." To describe Payson is simple: kind, gentle, thoughtful, and full of love, open-ended without condition. He is what every grandpa-type like me would want for a grandson.

The Red Wings gave me the idea for a present for Payson, as my memory floated back to Twin Lakes and the big bass that swam into the marshes in early spring, preparing to start the reproductive cycle once again.

Like so many of my other ventures in life, I decided to catch a trophy bass that required some special lures, lures that looked like a circus on a floating platform with hooks. Bass love big and gaudy presentations that look good to eat. Having grown up in trout country, my quest for a big bass became my own holy grail when I moved to North Idaho. I caught a few big ones, and nephew Kent and I went in search of this quarry on his visits to the North Country. My only real wall hanger was about four pounds, caught on little Hauser Lake west towards Spokane from the town of Rathdrum.

Three bass lures from my tackle box were selected for their beauty and success rate, as well as their value now as collectibles. Colleen and I made Payson a book of photos taken of him over the last three years, going from a lad of seven making lures to a ten-year-old hosting us at his birthday dinner. Payson sat next to me, guiding my order at the very noisy and crowded franchise steak joint, explaining what my order was when it arrived.

As I stroked his shoulder while he opened his present, the thought of the Ukraine war was not lost on me, and all the innocents suffering in this insanity. But this was here and now.

Payson was overjoyed with the lures and my stories of their past grandeur. He had to hear of each fish caught, and how hard they fought. His ten-year-old world brought back my own precious times on the water and the thrill of a big bass smacking a surface lure, often in a leap clear out of the water. For those of you who remember my stories of Payson, you may recall when I said to him one day, "Payson, you are going to be like Peter, the big fisherman from the Bible." He looked at me with a real, honest, questioning face and said, "Did he mostly catch trout?"

Recently, Payson's dad posted a picture on Facebook of him watching a fishing show, and a man tying a special knot. The photo had a quote above it: "If you know, you know!" How true. The kid lives and sleeps fishing; it consumes him. Already, he is talking of becoming a professional fisherman so he can fish more. As I think of things to become, it doesn't sound bad to me. Some of my best times in life have come from hearing Red Wings sing in the background, as a lure is attacked from the depths and a shining, slab-sided bass breaks the surface, to find glory in the sun.

# Sweet Surprises

Recently, I sent a card and short note to friends who had lost a mother and wife. I included one of my books, hoping to give them good memories of people we had known in our small North Idaho village. I expected to hear nothing back from them, as losses of family members bring up so many other things that need attention, attention that includes mending hearts of those still overwhelmed with grief. It is not easy, especially when one witnesses the loss of a loved one, inch by inch, over a long period of time. Your heart, and part of your consciousness, draws inward as time goes on, and as the light more clearly dims with each passing day.

Last night I received a long email from the husband, an old friend who has been in my life framed picture for almost fifty years. We first became acquainted when he was the manager of an office supply and bookstore in Sandpoint, Idaho. Mike is a tall, lean character. If you had asked central casting on a movie set to send you a bookstore owner from old London, he would have been the selection sans the accent. Always very proper and polite with sincerity, he worked at various professions, finally settling on insurance and was very good at it. For years, he handled our construction business coverage, keeping us up to date about necessary changes with his calm, reassuring nature.

The note was so profound—it captured every emotion one has on losing a spouse without saying it. He described the loss with the funeral flowers on the table along with other items, alluding to the empty space now felt in his heart and house. His note was poetry! Simple and pure, the kind a person writes when loss is still heavy on the mind and indelible in the nature of the day. I read it twice, saying to myself, "And others think they can write!" It was beautiful in every measure, referencing Elmore Leonard's ten rules of writing. Leonard added an eleventh rule later. "Write the book the way it should be written, then give it to somebody to put in the commas and shit." He also referenced my books, a reference I had to look up. It almost seemed too good for my writing, but I'm happy I said it. "Hoping to see the value in each day, remembering those we loved and lost…" What more is there worth saying?

Mike's note was so moving to me it has been in my thoughts since I first read it. Perhaps because we tend to overlook the hidden treasures so many folks bury when they are in a professional situation, a situation that may not lend itself to the depths they have to offer. In short, the old adage "Never judge a book by its cover" is apropos.

To me, the simple clarities are the best; long-winded eloquence is tedious and boring. If you must refer to a dictionary every five minutes to understand what the writer is saying, forget the writer! Life shouldn't be written as a textbook. It needs hardship, loss, humor, and love, along with pathos, redemption, and grandeur (when needed). Mike said in his note about my book, "It is the type of reading I need right now: rooted, earthy, real." And that, my friends, makes it all worthwhile.

Friend Dennis has repeatedly said to me, "Scott, it's the stories that count; you must write them down." I think of the great short story writers and remember a line Ms. White often spoke in my short story class at ISU: "Short stories are difficult, very difficult. You must be able to hold the reader while condensing an idea into a full, readable, informative, complete story." An incomplete list of the American masters are

Steinbeck, Saroyan, Thurber, Twain, Poe, and Hemingway. In reading their stories, Ms. White's quote comes true. I write my stories each week, hoping that they will do exactly what Mike quoted they did for him. I am gladdened when they have the same effect on someone else.

Stories need to be documented, told over and over again so as not to be lost as time presses on. Anyone can tell and write them. You don't need permission from your high school English teacher. I hear, almost daily, stories people pass on to me that would make for marvelous reading. When I express to the tellers, 'Write it down," reluctance comes across. "I can't write." Yes, you can! If it's not polished, seek help from a friend, because Dennis is right; "The stories are what counts."

My readers have taught me what is important. It's the narrative of the story; punctuation mechanics can be fixed later.

Photo: Colleen, Roger, and Ruth

## ROGER

In every tree the wind gives sound,
every grain of sand upon our feet
and every bee carrying out its
appointed rounds; he will be there.
The sun and waves warm high lake
shores with snow fields above, feeding
the future one drop at a time; he will be there.

Each flight of hurried wings and elk singing
from the hill, to the smallest of life, we
remember he saw the wonder, and he is there.
I marvel at sunrises knowing he loved their silence,
and in the sunsets, I see all those I have loved,
the colors clearer now; they wait beside him
beguiled, by that knowing, curious smile.

Love, Scott

Photo: Brixen, Colleen, Scott, and Buck

"May all your sunsets reflect on the natural world, giving promise to new adventure with the following sun. We are the sunsets and the sunrises too, and everything is within."

L. Scott Hancock

# About the Author

Author L. Scott Hancock

As most of my readers know, I was born and raised in Southeast Idaho, what natives call Yellowstone country. After college and some roaming, I took a job in North Idaho and built a life there for 45 years. Upon losing a wife to cancer, a friend and I decided it was time to come home. Come home to the big mountains and open skies of the west.

After moving to eastern Idaho in 2018, I found a wonderful new marriage and peace in the rivers, mountains, and animal kingdom of my youth.

Old friendships were rekindled, including with Gordon Perry, whom I have known for 64 years.

I want to thank, profoundly, Colleen, my wife, my first line of editorial comment. To Aaron Spickelmire, for his fastidious work, and to Kathi Irving, who, at the last minute, added her editorial skills which were greatly appreciated. Any changes back to western jargon and perhaps uncomfortable syntax are mine.

Lastly, I thank all the people that were a part of giving me the stories that make up this long, wonderful life.

Foot Note: Scott passed away on May 18, 2025, his fondest wish was to complete 6 books of his stories. I will do my best to make that happen for him.

Colleen Hancock

www.ingramcontent.com/pod-product-compliance
Lightning Source LLC
Chambersburg PA
CBHW052030030426
42337CB00027B/4938